Japanese Love Poems

Selections from the Manyōshū

Edited by
Evan Bates

DOVER PUBLICATIONS, INC.
Mineola, New York

Copyright

Bibliographical Note

This Dover edition, first published in 2005, is a new collection of poems selected from *The Manyōshū: One Thousand Poems Selected and Translated from the Japanese,* originally published in 1940 for the Nippon Gakujutsu Shinkokai by the Iwanami Shoten, Tokyo. This new anthology was prepared by Evan Bates, who also wrote an introductory Note for this edition.

Library of Congress Cataloging-in-Publication Data

Man'yåoshåu. English. Selections.
  Japanese love poems : selections from the Man'yåoshåu / edited by Evan Bates.
     p. cm.
  Originally published: Man'yåoshåu: one thousand poems selected and translated from the Japanese, Tokyo : published for the Nippon Gakujutsu Shinkåokai by the Iwanami Shoten, 1940.
  ISBN 0-486-44041-9 (pbk.)
  1. Waka—Translations into English. 2. Japanese poetry—To 794—Translations into English. 3. Love poetry, Japanese—Translations into English. I. Bates, Evan. II. Title.

PL758.15.A3 2005b
895.6'11—dc22

                                                                                    2005041345

Manufactured in the United States of America
Dover Publications, Inc., 31 East 2nd Street, Mineola, N.Y. 11501

Note

The poems in this volume have been selected from the Manyōshū, Japan's oldest poetry anthology and the most significant document of its early literary culture. The Manyoshu is extensive, comprising over 4,000 separate poems, and features contributions by members of all levels of society, including emperors, noble men and women, government officials, monks, soldiers, and peasants. The Manyō poets actually used Chinese characters to record their work (sometimes for meaning and sometimes for sound) even as their art, taken as a whole, began to define the new genre of Japanese literature. This period of uncharted literary territory brought about a manner of experimentation unique in Japanese history.

More than half of the poems in the Manyōshū can be considered to have love as a theme. The nearly 175 poems in our abridgement treat not only romantic love between youthful participants, but a myriad of human attachments and relationships: celebrations of married life; warning tales against infidelity and divorce; "story" poems telling of ill-fated competitions for spouses; memorials on the death of a spouse; and descriptions of tender love between family members. Many of the poems are written in the first person, but an interesting aspect of some texts is that they were composed at someone else's request or in the voice of someone else. For example, on page 56, the poet Ōtomo Yakamochi's wife requests that her husband compose a poem for her to give to her mother, who is travelling.

Japanese poetic form developed according to the limitations of the language itself: Japanese lacks the variety of sounds needed for interesting poetic rhyme and has minimal stress accents. Thus the primary characteristic that distinguishes its poetry from prose is the arrangement of syllables. Most of the poems in the Manyōshū are in the common *tanka* form—lines of 5-7-5-7-7 syllables—but there are also dialogues and other unusual forms. Particularly prized are the *choka* ("long poems"), which alternate lines of five and seven syllables and finish with an extra seven-syllable line. The choka was used in later poetry but the Manyō poets' mastery of the form was never surpassed. Many of the poems in the Manyōshū contain what are called "envoys" in our edition—stanzas appearing at the end of the poem that generally restate one or more of its themes.

In our volume, the name of each poet or group of poets is listed before each poem or series of poems. Descriptive texts of varying lengths appear in italics, in some cases before, and in some cases after, the poem to which they refer.

Japanese
Love Poems

Japanese Love Poems

EMPEROR YŪRYAKU

Your basket, with your pretty basket,
    Your trowel, with your little trowel,
Maiden, picking herbs on this hill-side,
I would ask you: Where is your home?
Will you not tell me your name?
Over the spacious Land of Yamato
It is I who reign so wide and far,
It is I who rule so wide and far.
I myself, as your lord, will tell you
Of my home, and my name.

EMPRESS KŌGYOKU

*Presented to the Emperor Jomei by
a messenger, Hashibito Oyu, on the occasion
of his hunting on the plain of Uchi*

From the age of the gods
    Men have been begotten and begetting;
They overflow this land of ours.
I see them go hither and thither
Like flights of teal—

1

But not you whom I love.
So I yearn each day till the day is over,
And each night till the dawn breaks;
Sleeplessly I pass this long, long night!

Envoys

Though men go in noisy multitudes
Like flights of teal over the mountain edge,
To me—oh what loneliness,
Since you are absent whom I love.

By the Toko Mountain in Ōmi
There flows the Isaya, River of Doubt.
I doubt whether now-a-days
You, too, still think of me?

EMPEROR TENJI

The Three Hills

Mount Kagu strove with Mount Miminashi
      For the love of Mount Unebi.
Such is love since the age of the gods;
As it was thus in the early days,
So people strive for spouses even now.

Envoys

When Mount Kagu and Mount Miminashi wrangled,
A god came over and saw it
Here—on this plain of Inami!

On the rich banner-like clouds
That rim the waste of waters
The evening sun is glowing,
And promises to-night
The moon in beauty!

EMPRESS IWA-NO-HIMÉ

Longing for the Emperor Nintoku

Since you, my Lord, were gone,
    Many long, long days have passed.
Should I now come to meet you
And seek you beyond the mountains,
Or still await you—await you ever?

Rather would I lay me down
On a steep hill's side,
And, with a rock for pillow, die,
Than live thus, my Lord,
With longing so deep for you.

Yes, I will live on
And wait for you,
Even till falls
On my long black waving hair
The hoar frost of age.

How shall my yearning ever cease—
Fade somewhere away,
As does the mist of morning
Shimmering across the autumn field
Over the ripening grain?

EMPRESS YAMATO-HIMÉ

*Presented to the Emperor Tenji
on the occasion of His Majesty's illness*

I turn and gaze far
    Towards the heavenly plains.
Lo, blest is my Sovereign Lord—
His long life overspans
The vast blue firmament.

[*After the death of the Emperor*]

Though my eyes could see your spirit soar
        Above the hills of green-bannered Kohata,
No more may I meet you face to face.

Others may cease to remember,
        But I cannot forget you—
Your beauteous phantom shape
Ever haunts my sight!

*On the occasion of the temporary enshrinement
of the Emperor Tenji*

On the vast lake of Ōmi
        You boatmen that come rowing
From the far waters,
And you boatmen that come rowing
Close by the shore,
Ply not too hard your oars in the far waters,
Ply not too hard your oars by the shore,
Lest you should startle into flight
The birds beloved of my dear husband!

PRINCE IKUSA

*Seeing the mountains when the Emperor Jomei
sojourned in Aya District, Sanuki Province*

Not knowing that the long spring day—
        The misty day—is spent,
Like the 'night-thrush' I grieve within me,
As sorely my heart aches.
Then across the hills where our Sovereign sojourns,
Luckily the breezes blow
And turn back my sleeves with morn and eve,
As I stay alone;
But, being on a journey, grass for pillow,
Brave man as I deem me,

I know not how to cast off
My heavy sorrows;
And like the salt-fires the fisher-girls
Burn on the shore of Ami,
I burn with the fire of longing
In my heart.

Envoy

Fitful gusts of wind are blowing
Across the mountain-range,
And night after night I lie alone,
Yearning for my love at home.

PRINCESS NUKADA

Yearning for the Emperor Tenji

While, waiting for you,
    My heart is filled with longing,
The autumn wind blows—
As if it were you—
Swaying the bamboo blinds of my door.

FUJIWARA KAMATARI

On the occasion of his marriage to Yasumiko, a palace attendant

Oh, Yasumiko I have won!
    Mine is she whom all men,
They say, have sought in vain.
Yasumiko I have won!

EMPRESS JITŌ

*Two poems said to have been composed by the Empress
after the death of the Emperor Temmu*

Even a flaming fire can be snatched,
    Wrapt and put in a bag—

Do they not say so?
But they say not that they know
How I may meet my Lord again!

Above the north mountain-range
That rims the blue firmament
The stars pass on,
The moon passes on—

PRINCE ŌTSU AND LADY ISHIKAWA

Waiting for you,
    In the dripping dew of the hill
I stood,—weary and wet
With the dripping dew of the hill.—*By the Prince*

Would I had been, beloved,
    The dripping dew of the hill,
That wetted you
While for me you waited.—*By the Lady*

PRINCESS ŌKU

    *Upon the departure of Prince Ōtsu for the capital
    after his secret visit to the Shrine of Isé*

To speed my brother
    Parting for Yamato,
In the deep of night I stood
Till wet with the dew of dawn.

The lonely autumn mountains
Are hard to pass over
Even when two go together—
How does my brother cross them all alone!

On her arrival at the capital after the death of Prince Ōtsu

Would that I had stayed
    In the land of Isé

Of the Divine Wind.
Why have I come
Now that he is dead!

Now that he is no more—
My dear brother—
Whom I so longed to see,
Why have I come,
Despite the tired horses!

PRINCESS TAJIMA

*Composed when Prince Hozumi was despatched by imperial
command to a mountain temple of Shiga in Ōmi*

Rather than stay behind to languish,
     I will come and overtake you—
Tie at each turn of your road
A guide-knot, my lord!

*Composed when her clandestine relations with Prince Hozumi
during her residence in the palace of Prince Takechi
became known*

Because of the slanderous tongues,
     The busy mouths abroad,
Now I cross the morning river
I have never crossed in my life before.

PRINCESS TAMOCHI

At the burial of Prince Kauchi in the Mirror Mountain in Toyo

Was it pleasing to my prince's soul?
     This Mirror Mountain in Toyo
He chose for his eternal palace.

In the Mirror Mountain in Toyo,
With its rock-doors shut,
Has he hidden himself?
However long I wait, he never returns.

O for strength to break the rock doors!
Weak woman that I am,
I know not what to do!

KAKINOMOTO HITOMARO

On leaving his wife as he set out from Iwami for the capital

Along the coast of Tsunu
    On the sea of Iwami
One may find no sheltering bay,
One may find no sequestered lagoon.
O well if there be no bay!
O well if there be no lagoon!
Upon Watazu's rocky strand,
Where I travel by the whale-haunted sea,
The wind blows in the morning,
And the waves wash at eve
The sleek sea-tangle and the ocean weed,
All limpid green.

Like the sea-tangle, swaying in the wave
Hither and thither, my wife would cling to me,
As she lay by my side.
Now I have left her, and journey on my way,
I look back a myriad times
At each turn of the road.
Farther and farther my home falls behind,
Steeper and steeper the mountains I have crossed.
My wife must be languishing
Like drooping summer grass.
I would see where she dwells—
Bend down, O mountains!

Envoys

From between the trees that grow
On Takatsunu's mountain-side
In the land of Iwami

I waved my sleeve to her—
Did she see me, my dear wife?

The leaves of bamboo grass
Fill all the hill-side
With loud rustling sounds;
But I think only of my love,
Having left her behind.

In the sea of Iwami,
　　By the cape of Kara,
There amid the stones under sea
Grows the deep-sea *miru* weed;
There along the rocky strand
Grows the sleek sea-tangle.

Like the swaying sea-tangle,
Unresisting would she lie beside me—
My wife whom I love with a love
Deep as the *miru*-growing ocean.
But few are the nights
We two have lain together.

Away I have come, parting from her
Even as the creeping vines do part.
My heart aches within me;
I turn back to gaze—
But because of the yellow leaves
Of Watari Hill,
Flying and fluttering in the air,
I cannot see plainly
My wife waving her sleeve to me.
Now as the moon, sailing through the cloud rift
Above the mountain of Yakami,
Disappears, leaving me full of regret,
So vanishes my love out of sight;
Now sinks at last the sun,
Coursing down the western sky.

I thought myself a strong man,
But the sleeves of my garment
Are wetted through with tears.

Envoys

My black steed
Galloping fast,
Away have I come,
Leaving under distant skies
The dwelling-place of my love.

Oh, yellow leaves
Falling on the autumn hill,
Cease a while
To fly and flutter in the air
That I may see my love's dwelling-place!

Presented to Princess Hatsusebé and Prince Osakabé

Dainty water-weeds, growing up-stream
    In the river of the bird-flying Asuka,
Drift down-stream, gracefully swaying.
Like the water-weeds the two would bend
Each toward the other, the princess and her consort.

But now no longer can she sleep,
With his fine smooth body clinging
Close to hers like a guardian sword.
Desolate must be her couch at night.
Unable to assuage her grief,
But in the hope of finding him by chance,
She journeys to the wide plain of Ochinu,
There, her skirt drenched with morning dew
And her coat soaked with the fog of evening,
She passes the night—a wayfarer with grass for pillow—
Because of him whom she nevermore will meet!

Envoy

Her lord and husband with whom she had slept,
The sleeves of their robes overlapping,
Has passed away to the plain of Ochinu.
How can she ever meet him again!

On the occasion of the temporary enshrinement of Princess Asuka

Across the river of the bird-flying Asuka
    Stepping-stones are laid in the upper shallows,
And a plank bridge over the lower shallows.
The water-frond waving along the stones,
Though dead, will reappear.
The river-tresses swaying by the bridge
Wither, but they sprout again.

How is it, O Princess, that you have
Forgotten the morning bower
And forsaken the evening bower
Of him, your good lord and husband—
You who did stand handsome like a water-frond,
And who would lie with him,
Entwined like tender river-tresses?

No more can he greet you.
You make your eternal abode
At the Palace of Kinohé whither oft in your lifetime
He and you made holiday together,
Bedecked with flowers in spring,
Or with golden leaves in autumn-tide,
Walking hand in hand, your eyes
Fondly fixed upon your lord as upon a mirror,
Admiring him ever like the glorious moon.

So it may well be that grieving beyond measure,
And moaning like a bird unmated,
He seeks your grave each morn.
I see him go, drooping like summer grass,
Wander here and there like the evening-star,
And waver as a ship wavers in the sea.

No heart have I to comfort him,
Nor know I what to do.
Only your name and your deathless fame,
Let me remember to the end of time;
Let the Asuka River, your namesake,
Bear your memory for ages,
O Princess adored!

Envoys

Even the flowing water
Of the Asuka River—
If a weir were built,
Would it not stand still?

O Asuka, River of To-morrow,
As if I thought that I should see
My Princess on the morrow,
Her name always lives in my mind.

After the death of his wife

Since in Karu lived my wife,
    I wished to be with her to my heart's content;
But I could not visit her constantly
Because of the many watching eyes—
Men would know of our troth,
Had I sought her too often
So our love remained secret like a rock-pent pool;
I cherished her in my heart,
Looking to after-time when we should be together,
And lived secure in my trust
As one riding a great ship.
Suddenly there came a messenger
Who told me she was dead—
Was gone like a yellow leaf of autumn.
Dead as the day dies with the setting sun,
Lost as the bright moon is lost behind the cloud,

Alas, she is no more, whose soul
Was bent to mine like the bending seaweed!

When the word was brought to me
I knew not what to do nor what to say;
But restless at the mere news,
And hoping to heal my grief
Even a thousandth part,
I journeyed to Karu and searched the market-place
Where my wife was wont to go!

There I stood and listened,
But no voice of her I heard,
Though the birds sang in the Unebi Mountain;
None passed by, who even looked like my wife.
I could only call her name and wave my sleeve.

Envoys

In the autumn mountains
The yellow leaves are so thick.
Alas, how shall I seek my love
Who has wandered away?—
I know not the mountain track.

I see the messenger come
As the yellow leaves are falling.
Oh, well I remember
How on such a day we used to meet—
My wife and I!

In the days when my wife lived,
     We went out to the embankment near by—
We two, hand in hand—
To view the elm-trees standing there
With their outspreading branches
Thick with spring leaves. Abundant as their greenery
Was my love. On her leaned my soul.
But who evades mortality?—
One morning she was gone, flown like an early bird.

Clad in a heavenly scarf of white,
To the wide fields where the shimmering *kagerō** rises
She went and vanished like the setting sun.

The little babe—the keepsake
My wife has left me—
Cries and clamours.
I have nothing to give; I pick up the child
And clasp it in my arms.
In her chamber, where our two pillows lie,
Where we two used to sleep together,
Days I spend alone, broken-hearted:
Nights I pass, sighing till dawn.

Though I grieve, there is no help;
Vainly I long to see her.
Men tell me that my wife is
In the mountains of Hagai—
Thither I go,
Toiling along the stony path;
But it avails me not,
For of my wife, as she lived in this world,
I find not the faintest shadow.

Envoys

To-night the autumn moon shines—
The moon that shone a year ago,
But my wife and I who watched it then together
Are divided by ever-widening wastes of time.

When leaving my love behind
In the Hikité mountains—
Leaving her there in her grave,
I walk down the mountain path,
I feel not like one living.

---

*Kagerō, the quivering appearance of the air rising from the hot surface of the
ground.

On the death of an unemé from Tsu, Kibi Province*

Beauty was hers that glowed like autumn mountains
And grace as of the swaying bamboo stem.
How was it that she died—she who should have lived
A life long as the coil of *taku* rope,
Though the dew falls at morn
To perish at dusk,
Though the mists that rise at eve
Vanish with the daybreak.
On learning her fate I grieve—
I who saw her but casually.
But her husband, tender as young grass,
Who with her soft white arm for pillow
Lay at her side close like a guardian sword—
How lonely must he lie—he in his widowed bed!
What anguish must fill his love-lorn heart,
Yearning for her who all too soon has gone—
Like morning dew—like mists of evening!

Envoys

How sorrowful to see
The road across the river-shallows
By which departed the lady
Of Shigatsu of Sasanami!

When we met, I only took—
And how I regret it now!—
A vague careless glance
At the lady of Ōtsu.

---

*An *unemé* (young woman serving at court, chiefly at the imperial table, selected
from among the daughters of influential families or of higher officials in the
provinces) was known by the name of the place and province from which she
came.

At the cremation of the Maiden of Hijikata on the hills of Hatsusé

The cloud drifting over the brows
     Of the hills of secluded Hatsusé—
Can it, alas, be she?

Though my thoughts of her
     Grow a hundredfold in my heart
Like the leaves of the crinum
On the sea-coast of Kumanu,
I do not meet her face to face.

Did men living long ago
     Pass also sleepless nights like me,
Longing for their beloved?

Lamenting his own fate as he was about to die
in the land of Iwami

All unaware, it may be,
     That I lie in Kamo-yama,
Pillowed on a rock,
She is waiting now—my wife—
Waiting for my return.

YOSAMI, WIFE OF HITOMARO

On parting from Hitomaro

Though you say, 'Do not grieve!'
     I know not, alas,
When we shall meet again;
How can I but pine after you?

On the death of Hitomaro

Day in, day out,
     I wait for my husband—

Alas! he lies buried, men say,
In the ravine of the Stone River.

There can be no meeting
Face to face with him.
Arise, O clouds,
Hover above the Stone River
That I may watch and remember!

FROM THE "HITOMARO COLLECTION"

During the journey

I would quickly reach my loved one's dwelling
    That stands far away under the clouds;
Hasten, my black steed!

Presented to Prince Yugé

The night hours have advanced,
    It must be the dead of night:
In the sky where the wild geese call
I see the moon travelling on.

Kagu-yama,
    The Heavenly Hill afar,
Is misted over this evening—
Spring is here!

Over the branches of the cryptomerias,
    Planted, perhaps, by men of old,
There hangs a trailing mist—
Spring has come!

While I wait and long for you, my loved one,
    I hear the boat crossing the River of Heaven—
The sound of the oars
Echoing over the waters of night.

Love in autumn

Debate not who I am,
        Say neither this nor that
Of me who, drenched
In September's chilling dew,
Await my dear love's coming!

'Reaper on the Suminoé fields,
        Have you no servants?'
'Servants I have; yet for my love
I labour on her private ground."

This is the cloth I wove for my lord
        With weary hands;
When the spring comes round,
In what colours shall I print it?

The lasses dance and tread the ground for the new house
        And the jewels of their bracelets jingle;
That lad who sparkles as the jewels,
Ask him to come in!

O that she might rather die
        Whom I cherish in my heart!
Even when she lives,
None says she will be mine.

You start so early this morning
        The dewy grass will wet your leg-ties;
I, too, out so early,
Will gladly dip the hem of my skirt.

 Since I left the loving hands of my mother,
        Never once have I known
Such helplessness in my heart!

Let none, born after me,
        Ever, ever meet, as I did,
Such ways of love!

I have lost a true man's mettle,
        Day to night and night to day
I waste with thoughts of love.

People throng the sun-lit Palace-road,
        Yet, you—and you alone—
Are my heart's desire!

Strong man as I am,
        Who force my way even through the rocks,
In love I rue in misery.

As if to say that I may die
        If I die of love for her,
That cruel girl now passes
The front-gate of my house.

Poems of love referring to various things

How named is the god
        Whom I would entreat with offerings,
That I may meet my love,
If but in dream?

Should the time come
        When the names of heaven and earth per-
ish,
Then, then alone we should cease to meet!

O that the hill, the stony road,
        Were removed from your way hither;
Your horse will stumble,
While I wait for you.

Over Kohata, the hill in Yamashina,
        I can get a horse to ride,
Yet on foot I have come,
Driven by stress of love for you!

My life vanishing
      Like the numbers written on water,
I have appealed to the gods with vows
That I may meet my love.

The great earth itself
      Might be exhausted by digging,
But of love alone in this world
Could we never reach the end!

Sleepless with longing for my love,
      Now I see the morning break;
O the mandarin-ducks flying by—
Are they the couriers from my girl?

Like the silkworm in the cocoon
      Which her loving mother rears,
That maid so close secluded in her home—
O for the means of seeing her!

As the *yū*-cloth is dyed fast and deep
      Which ties the forelock of the men
In the land of Hi,
So is my heart coloured with love;
How can I forget?

Now that I have uttered my name
      Clear as the famous call
Of a Hayahito on his night-watch round,
Trust me as your wife, my lord!

I will tread the sharpness of the double-edged sword
      And die with a good heart,
If it be for your sake.

How plainly one may see
      The new road now they make!
So plainly have I heard
Everything about you, dear girl.

Dialogue poem

If the thunder rolls for a while
    And the sky is clouded, bringing rain,
Then you will stay beside me.

Even when no thunder sounds
    And no rain falls, if you but ask me,
Then I will stay beside you.

LADY ISHIKAWA

Addressed to Ōtomo Sukunamaro

Old, old woman that I am,
    How could I have sunk so deep in love,
Like a helpless child!

LADY ISHIKAWA AND ŌTOMO TANUSHI

I heard that you were
    A gallant courtier,
Yet you refused me shelter and sent me away—
How boorish of the gallant courtier!—*By Ishikawa*

Ōtomo Tanushi was known by the name of Chūrō. He was very good-looking, and his manners were courtly beyond comparison, wherefore he was admired by all who saw, or heard of him. There was a certain young woman, named Ishikawa, who, wishing to live with him, was ever lamenting her solitude. She desired to write him a note, but there was no favourable opportunity to send it. Thereupon, she devised a plan. Disguising herself as a humble old woman, and carrying a pail with her, she went near his bedchamber, where she squatted and rapped on the door, and said in a hoarse voice that she was a poor woman of the neighbourhood who had come to beg for fire. Chūrō in the darkness did not discover the fraud. The girl, disappointed at the failure of her artifice, took all the fire she wanted, and thereafter went away. Next

*morning, ashamed of her own misbehaviour but indignant at the
frustration of her heart's desire, she indited this poem, which she
sent him in order to mock at him.*

A gallant courtier,
     I am, indeed;
A gallant courtier am I,
Who refused you shelter and sent you away!—*By Ōtomo Tanushi*

Furu Tamuké

Leaving the province of Tsukushi

Would my love were a bracelet!
     Tying her to my left arm,
I would start on my journey!

Mikata Shami and his Wife

*Composed during an illness of Mikata shortly after his marriage
to a daughter of Sono Ikuha*

If tied, it would slip off;
     And untied, it was too long,—
Ah, that hair of yours!—
Is it all disarranged
Now while I see you not?—*By Mikata*

'Do it up!'
     'It is now so long!'
So say they all.
But as you saw it, I will keep
This hair of mine, dishevelled though it be.—*By his wife*

In the city square
     Men come and go, treading
On the orange-tree shadows;
My thoughts turn a thousand ways
When I see you not, beloved.—*By Mikata*

WIFE OF GO DAN-OCHI

Composed during her husband's journey to Isé

Breaking and spreading for a bed
    The shore reeds of Isé of the Divine Wind,
Does he, my husband, sleep a traveller's sleep—
On that lonely rugged sea-coast?

ANONYMOUS

The Old Bamboo-Cutter

Once upon a time there lived an old man. He was called 'Old Bamboo-Cutter' (Taketori no Oji). In the last month of spring he went up a hill to view the country-side. Suddenly he discovered nine girls who were cooking soup, and who were all possessed of an unrivalled beauty and charm. One of the damsels called to the old man, laughed and said: 'Uncle, come blow up the fire under the kettle!' 'Very well, very well,' he replied. Hobbling slowly, he reached the spot where the girls were, and seated himself among them. After a while, all the girls, with smiles on their faces, began to question one another, saying, 'Who called this old man?' Thereupon the Bamboo-Cutter apologized and said, 'Most unexpectedly I have met you fairy maidens. My mind is perplexed beyond endurance. Let me redeem with a poem the offence of having intruded myself upon your company!' So saying, he made the following poem and envoys.

When I was a new-born babe
    My mother carried me in her arms;
When an infant still tied with a band
To the back of my nurse, I wore
A sleeveless gown with lining sewed in;
When a boy with hair trimmed at the neck
I was clad in a dappled robe with sleeves.
At the age of you dear maidens
My hair was black as the bowels of a mud-snail.
I would comb it down to the shoulders,
Or have it bound up in knots
Or sometimes let it hang loose like a boy.

I had a vest of thin silk with large woven figures
Of purple matching well with its reddish tint,
And a robe of a fabric dyed with the *hagi*-flower
Of Tōzato Onu in Suminoé,
To which was attached a cord of *Koma* brocade—
These I wore one over the other.

There was the cloth of *tahé* tissue
And the hand-woven cloth of sun-dried hemp,
Made with rare skill by girl hemp-spinners
And by girls who were treasured like precious robes;
When I put these on together like a double skirt,
Many a country lass from her lowly cottage
Would come, asking me to marry her.

The double-patterned stockings from a far country,
And the shoes fashioned by the men of Asuka,
Shunning the damp of the rainy season,—
I would put them on and stand under the eaves;
Then maidens who had heard of me somewhere,
Would come to me, bidding me not to walk away.

I would arrange my silken girdle of azure
In the manner of a *Kara* girdle like a pendant sash,
And so bedeck my waist slim as a wasp
Flying above the tiled roof of the Sea God's Temple;
Then would I hang up clear mirrors side by side,
And turn back to them again and again
To see my face therein.
When in spring I sauntered forth afield,
The pheasants of the moor, delighting in me,
Came flying and crowing merrily.
When I were to the hills in autumn
The enamoured clouds of heaven hovered low above me.
When I started for home, all along the way
The gay ladies of the palace and the court gallants
Would all look back on me in admiration,
And ask one another, saying, 'Who is he?'
So did I do and live in days gone by.

Though to-day you dear damsels may wonder
Who I am and say: 'We don't know the man,'
I was once the talk of the town—
Thus did I do and live in days gone by.

Did not the wise man of ancient times
Bring back, to set an example for after ages,
The cart in which the old man was sent away?

Envoys

Can it be that grey hair
Will never grow on you maidens
If you live long, unless death
Spares you from seeing it?

When grey hair has grown
On you, may it not be then
That you too will be mocked
By young folk as I am now?

Replies by the maidens

The dear old man's verse
        Has stunned us,
We fairy maidens nine—
Are we humbled by his word?

My shame I will bear,
        My shame I will ignore;
And before he speaks another word,
To his counsel mutely will I yield.

Shall I be false to friends
        To whose hearts mine is bound
In life and death?
To his counsel I also will yield.

ANONYMOUS

From Mount Kaminabi of Mimoro
    Clouds overshadow the sky,
Bringing heavy rain;
The rain is swept in spray
And the storm gathers.

Has he reached home,
He who went back
Across the great-mouthed Wolf's Moor,
Deep in thoughts of me?

Envoy

Troubled with thoughts of him,
Who had gone from me,
I, too, could not sleep
The whole night through.

EMPRESS KŌMYŌ

To the Emperor Shōmu

How gladdening would be this falling snow,
    Could I but watch with you, my husband!

PRINCE TONERI AND A MAIDEN

'Shame it is,' I say and sigh,
    'For a strong man to love unloved!'
Yet so do I love—wretched that I am.—*By the Prince*

Now I know—
    For a strong man
Loveth and sigheth—
Why my hair-cord is wet.—*By the Maiden*

PRINCE HOZUMI

Ah, that rascal love
    I have put away at home,
Locked in a coffer—
Here he comes, pouncing on me!

*The above was a favourite poem of Prince Hozumi, who used al-
ways to recite it at banquets when the merry-making was at its
height.*

PRINCESS KI

Even the wild-ducks skimming
    By the shore of the pond of Karu
Do not sleep alone
On the dainty water-weeds!

PRINCE YUHARA

Addressed to a young woman

What can I do with you—
    You who so resemble
The laurel in the moon
That I see with my eyes
But cannot touch with my hands?

PRINCE YUHARA AND AN ANONYMOUS PERSON

By the light of the Moon God
    Come to me, dear heart!
No mountain walls divide us—
The way is not long.—*By the Prince*

Reply

Though clear and bright
    The Moon God lights the way,

So blind am I with love,
I feel I cannot reach you.

PRINCE AKI

On an imperial visit to the province of Isé

Would that they were flowers,
    The white surges far upon the sea of Isé—
I would wrap and bring them home
As a souvenir for my beloved wife.

Oh, my dear love far away!
    Because you are not here,
And the way is distant,
Restless is my heart with longing;
My grieving heart knows no respite.
Oh, were I the cloud that sails the sky!
Oh, were I a high-flying bird!
To-morrow I would go and speak to you.
Then you, my love, untroubled for my sake,
And for your sake I myself untroubled,
We would live together even now
A happy pair as ever.

Envoy

No longer do I sleep
With your dainty arm for pillow.
Meantime a year has passed away—
To think of it, alas!—
Without my seeing you.

PRINCE ICHIHARA

Peerless are the gems
    That I wear on my locks;

Such are you to me,
And my heart moves at your will.

PRINCE NAGAYA

*Composed when the Emperor Mommu visited
the Pleasure-Palace of Yoshinu*

The morning air is cold on Mount Ujima,
      Now that I travel far from my beloved
Who would offer me clothing.

PRINCE KADOBÉ

Viewing the trees in the streets at the Eastern Market

I have not met her for so long
      That the street-trees at the Eastern Market
Let droop their branches low—
Well may I languish for love of her!

PRINCESS TAKATA

To Prince Imaki

This world is so full
      Of men with slanderous tongues.
May we not meet in the life to come—
If we may not now, my dearest?

PRINCESS HIROKAWA

The sheaves of my love-thoughts
      Would fill seven carts—
Carts huge and heavy-wheeled.
Such a burden I bear
Of my own choice.

I thought there could be
    No more love left anywhere.
Whence then is come this love,
That has caught me now
And holds me in its grasp?

TAJIHI KASAMARO

On his journey to Tsukushi

By the sea-shore of Mitsu, that reminds one
    Of the mirror standing on a girl's comb-case,
I linger, longing for my wife, and sleep alone,
My scarlet sash untied.
I can but weep aloud like the crane crying
In the morning mist at the twilight hour of dawn.
Seeking to relieve me of my sorrow,
If only by a thousandth part,
I go out to gaze toward my home,
Which is—alas!—lost in the white clouds,
That trail across the green mountain of Kazuraki.

I journey on to the far-off land—
Passing Awaji Island now lying before,
And leaving behind me the island of Awashima.
I hear the shouts of sailors in the morning calm,
And in the calm of evening the plash of oars.
Labouring over the waves,
Circling about amid the rocks,
And past the beach of Inabizuma,
I wander on like a bird
Till Ié-no-shima, the 'Home Island,' comes into sight,
Where thick and swaying on the stony shore
Grows the weed men call 'Speak-not'—
Ah, why have I come away from my wife
Without a word of farewell?

Envoy

Would that my wife and I,
Unfastening our girdles for each other
And with our snow-white sleeves overlapping,
Had reckoned the day of my return
Before I came away upon my journey!

TAJIHI YANUSHI

Her husband is gone towards Naniwa;
        Pity it is to see a young wife,
Left gathering spring herbs!

TAJIHI—

An old threnody

The mallards call with evening from the reeds
        And float with dawn midway on the water;
They sleep with their mates, it is said,
With white wings overlapping and tails a-sweep
Lest the frost should fall upon them.

As the stream that flows never returns,
And as the wind that blows is never seen,
My wife, of this world, has left me,
Gone I know not whither!
So here, on the sleeves of these clothes
She used to have me wear,
I sleep now all alone!

Envoy

Cranes call flying to the reedy shore;
How desolate I remain
As I sleep alone!

   This poem was composed in grief at the death of his wife.

KASA KANAMURA

Composed at the request of a young lady for sending to a member
of the Emperor's retinue on a journey to Ki, in winter,
in the tenth month of the first year of Jinki (724)

You, dear husband, who have gone forth
    With the many men of eighty clans
Accompanying the Emperor on his journey—

You who went by the highway of Karu,
Admiring the view of the Unebi Mountain,
And now having entered the province of Ki
Are crossing, perhaps, the mountain of Matsuchi—

You may find your journey a pleasant thing,
As you watch the autumn leaves fly and scatter,
Yet never a tender thought give to me.
Though this may be an empty fear,
I cannot stay at peace at all.
A thousand times over I wish
To follow you on your track.
And yet, young and helpless girl that I am,
I should not know what answer to give,
If a road-guard should challenge me—
So here I stand, faltering.

Envoys

Rather than remain behind
To pine after you,
I would we were the Imo-Sé Mountains of Ki—
The 'Man and Wife' for ever.

If I go seeking after you,
Following your footmarks,
Will the guard of the pass
In Ki bid me halt?

On winning the love of a maiden during the Emperor's visit
to the Detached Palace at Mika-no-hara, in spring,
in the third month of the second year of Jinki (725)

A sojourner in Mika's plains,
    I saw you on the road,
A stranger to me like a cloud of heaven:
The words I could not speak to you,
Quite choked my heart.
Yet we two, by the mercy of the gods,
Are now wedded in love and trust,
Lying upon each other's sleeve.
Ah, to-night! Would it were as long
As a hundred autumn nights together!

Envoys

I have leaned, body and soul,
Towards you, beloved,
From the moment I saw you—
A stranger like a cloud of heaven.

Unable to bear the thought
That to-night will quickly pass,
Oh, how I pray that it might be
Long as a hundred autumn nights!

On the occasion of the Sovereign's journey to Inami District,
Harima Province, in autumn, on the fifteenth
of the ninth month of the third year of Jinki (726)

On Matsuho's shore of Awaji Island,
    Seen yonder from Funasé of Nakisumi,
There are fisher-maids, I am told,
Who cut the dainty seaweed in the morning calm,
And in the evening calm burn salt-fires.
But I, knowing not how to reach them,
And deprived of my manly courage,
Am maid-like distraught with sorrow,

And wander about yearning for the far beach—
Helpless without boat and oar!

Envoys

O that I had boat and oar
That I might visit those fisher-maids
Cutting the dainty seaweed!—
I would go, however high the waves might be.

Could I ever weary of watching,
Walking back and forth interminably,
The white waves that ceaselessly break
On Funasé's beach of Nakisumi?

LADY KASA

To Ōtomo Yakamochi

In the loneliness of my heart
    I feel as if I should perish
Like the pale dew-drop
Upon the grass of my garden
In the gathering shades of twilight.

Even the sands uncounted of a long beach
    That takes eight hundred days to travel—
Could they at all outnumber
My thoughts of love,
O guardian of the isle on the sea?

Oh how steadily I love you—
    You who awe me
Like the thunderous waves
That lash the sea-coast of Isé!

More sad thoughts crowd into my mind
    When evening comes; for then
Appears your phantom shape—
Speaking as I have known you speak.

If it were death to love,
  I should have died—
And died again
One thousand times over.

I dreamed I was holding
  A double-edged sword close to my body—
What does it foretell? It tells
That I shall meet you soon.

If the gods of heaven and earth
  Were bereft of reason,
I might die
Without seeing you
Whom I love so well.

The bells are tolling,
  Bidding all to rest.
But you being for ever on my mind,
I cannot sleep.

To love you who love me not
  Is like going to a great temple
To bow in adoration
Behind the back of the famished devil.

TAKAHASHI—

  An elegy on the death of his wife

Till my black hair be white,
  We shall be together, I and my darling,
Sleeping, our sleeves overlapped,
She nestling by my side,
Bound in never-ending love,
Through this new age of our Sovereign;
So I vowed, but my word proved false,
My hopes were vain.
She has gone from me and our loved home,

Leaving a crying child,
And faded like a morning mist,
Vanished among the Sagaraka Hills
Of Yamashiro.
I know not what to say, nor what to do.
But out of the room we slept in
I come at morn, thinking of my wife,
With evening I go back and grieve.
When my precious child cries,
Helpless man as I am—
I bear him on my back or in my arms;
And ceaselessly I weep, as sings the morning bird,
Longing for her in vain;
And, though dumb the hills that bind her,
I gaze upon them as my heart's resort!

Envoys

Changing is this world of ours;
Those hills, cold to my heart,
I now must gaze upon
As my heart's resort!

I cannot but weep aloud
And ceaselessly, as sings the morning bird,
Since no way remains to me
To regain my love!

KURAMOCHI CHITOSÉ

As one but hears the rumbling thunder,
        So had I only heard of fair Yoshinu—
And how that name rang in my wistful ears!
There on the mountain with trees overgrown
I stand to gaze below.
The morning mist rises everywhere
From the river shallows as day breaks,
And there the song-frogs chirp in the evening.
O what a pity that, being on a journey
And even obliged to sleep in my clothes,

I must alone without you, love,
Look on this clean and beautiful river-beach!

Envoy

Mount Mifuné above the cascades
Overawes me by its grandeur,
Yet never for a day, nor for a moment,
Do I forget you, my love!

WIFE OF KURAMOCHI—

To a long absent husband

I am sick body and soul
     Because not even a messenger comes
To bring me word of you,
My husband ruddy-cheeked.
Pray not to the gods,
Nor call in the diviner
To burn the tortoise-shell!
It is love that torments me:
The pain pierces me to the bone,
And grief has broken my heart.
My life is fast ebbing towards its end.
Who calls me now?—

Is it you, sweet husband of mine,
Or is it my dear mother?
In vain you seek at the cross-roads
The oracle of evening and of the way
For the sake of me who must die!

Envoys

Though they ask the diviner,
And seek oracles at the cross-roads,
There is no finding
The means to see you.

Not that I cared for my life—
But just because of you,
Sweet husband of mine,
Have I wished to live on.

It is said that there was a young woman (her surname was Kuramochi), whose husband had deserted her for many years. Pining after him, she was taken ill. Growing weaker and more wasted every day, she suddenly faced death. Thereupon, she sent for her husband; she then recited the above poems with sobs and tears. She died shortly after.

FUJIWARA HIROTSUGU AND A YOUNG LADY

Poem sent with cherry-flowers to a young lady by Fujiwara Hirotsugu

Slight not these flowers!
    Each single petal contains
A hundred words of mine.

Reply by the young lady

Were these flowers broken off,
    Unable to hold in each petal
A hundred words of yours?

ABÉ OKINA

Poem of sorrow addressed to his mother when he was despatched to China

My love for you, O mother,
    Is endless like the bounds of heaven
Where the clouds drift on and on,
But the day I must leave you
Now draws near!

NAKATOMI YAKAMORI AND A MAIDEN SANU CHIGAMI

Poems exchanged while Yakamori lived in exile

O for a fire from heaven
   To haul, fold and burn up
The long-stretched road you go!—*By the Maiden, on parting*

Were it not for the dresses
   You gave me as a keepsake,
How, beloved, could I
Live the days of my life?—*By Yakamori*

A strange land is hard to live in, men say;
   Come quickly home,
Before I die of love for you!—*By the Maiden*

Within the bounds of heaven and earth
   None, none you can find
Who loves you as I!—*By the Maiden*

These are the clothes your dainty girl,
   Bowed in thought, has sewn—
A keepsake for the day
When we shall meet again.—*By the Maiden*

Do the courtiers even now
   Delight in nothing
But teasing and mockery?—*By Yakamori*

Though I try to calm down my soul
   By prayers night and morning,
My heart aches
With overwhelming love.—*By the Maiden*

'A lord returning home
   Has come,' said they—
And I well-nigh swooned,
Thinking it was you.—*By the Maiden*

For the time that you return,
    I will guard my life, my lord;
O forget me not!—*By the Maiden*

Even to-day, were I in the City,
    I would be standing
Outside the western royal stables,
Breathless to see you.—*By Yakamori*

LADY ABÉ

I shall think of nothing more now.
    To you I have yielded, my dear;
Upon you my soul leans.

Think not of things, my beloved!
Have you not me—who would go,
If need be, through fire and flood for you?

My very soul, it seems,
    Has stolen into every stitch
Of the robe you wear.

LADY HEGURI

*Sent to Ōtomo Yakamochi, Governor of Etchū,
    by occasional posts*

Gazing at the hand you squeezed
    When we were heart to heart,
Pledging the love of a myriad years,
I am overwhelmed with longing.

The pine bloom, though you overlook it
    Among the mass of blossoms,
Blows now in vain.

ŌTOMO TABITO

*Remembering his deceased wife: composed in the fifth year of
Jinki (728), when he was Governor-General of the Dazaifu*

Some weeks after her death

My dear wife loved my arm,
    Her pillow, to sleep on;
Now I have none like her,
To sleep upon it.

Starting on his journey to the capital

When I sleep alone, in the Imperial City,
    In my long forsaken house,
How much more painful that will be
Than ever on my journey!

*Composed during his journey from the Dazaifu to the capital,
in winter, in the twelfth month of the second year
of Tempyō (730)*

Passing the shore of Tomo

My darling gazed at the juniper
    On the shore of Tomo;
It stands, flourishing as ever,
But she who saw it is dead.

O Juniper, that grasps the rocks of the beach
    With ancient roots,
If I ask where she is, she who saw you,
Can you answer me?

Passing the cape of Minumé

Together with my wife I passed
    This lovely cape Minumé;
Now on my lonely voyage home
I see it and I weep.

When last I journeyed down,
    We two admired this cape;
Now I am filled with sadness,
Passing it all alone.

On reaching his residence

My house forsaken by my love,
    And so desolate—
How much more it pains my heart
Than did my travels, grass for pillow!

This garden which I, together with my darling,
Laid out and planted,
Has now grown waste and rife
With tall and wild-boughed trees!

Each time I see this plum-tree,
Which my darling planted,
My heart swells with sadness
And tears fill my eyes.

ŌTOMO SUKUNAMARO

She goes to the sun-bright palace;
    Yet so dear to me is the maiden,
It is heart-ache to keep her,
But despair to let her go.

LADY ŌTOMO OF SAKANOÉ

Reply to Fujiwara Maro

Even if you say, 'I come,'
    At times you will not come.
Now you say: 'I will not come.'
Why should I look for your coming—
When you say you will not come!

Love's complaint

At wave-bright Naniwa
    The sedges grow, firm-rooted—
Firm were the words you spoke,
And tender, pledging me your love,
That it would endure through all the years;
And to you I yielded my heart,
Spotless as a polished mirror.
Never, from that day, like the sea-weed
That sways to and fro with the waves,
Have I faltered in my fidelity,
But have trusted in you as in a great ship.
Is it the gods who have divided us?
Is it mortal men who intervene?
You come no more, who came so often,
Nor yet arrives a messenger with your letter.
There is—alas!—nothing I can do.
Though I sorrow the black night through
And all day till the red sun sinks,
It avails me nothing. Though I pine,
I know not how to soothe my heart's pain.
Truly men call us 'weak women.'
Crying like an infant,
And lingering around, I must still wait,
Wait impatiently for a message from you!

Envoy

If from the beginning
You had not made me trust you,
Speaking of long, long years,
Should I have known now
Such sorrow as this?

Do you desire our love to endure?
    Then, if only while I see you
After days of longing and yearning,

Pray, speak to me
Sweet words—all you can!

As if a cloud were sailing
        Across the green mountain-side,
Do not smile to yourself too frankly,
Lest others should know of our love!

*Sent from her country estate of Tomi to her eldest daughter
remaining at home*

Dear child, my daughter, who stood
        Sadly musing by the gate
Though I was leaving for no foreign land,
I think of you day and night
And my body is become lean;
My sleeves, too, are tear-soaked with weeping.
If I must long for you so wretchedly,
I fear I cannot stay these many months
Here at this dreary old farm.

Envoy

Because you long for me so much—
Your sad thoughts all confused
Like the tangles of your morning hair—
I see you, dear child, in dream.

*Given to her nephew, Yakamochi, as he left her house
at Saho for his Western Residence*

The garment is thin
        That my loved one wears—
O Saho wind, blow not too hard
Until he reaches his home!

Feasting with her kinsfolk

Oh, the pain of my love that you know not—
    A love like the maiden-lily
Blooming in the thicket of the summer moor!

Sent to her elder daughter from the capital

I cherished you, my darling,
    As the Sea God the pearls
He treasures in his comb-box.
But you, led by your lord husband—
Such is the way of the world—
And torn from me like a vine,
Left for distant Koshi;
Since then, your lovely eyebrows
Curving like the far-off waves,
Ever linger in my eyes,
My heart unsteady as a rocking boat;
Under such a longing
I, now weak with age,
Come near to breaking.

Envoy

If I had foreknown such longing,
I would have lived with you,
Gazing on you every hour of the day
As in a shining mirror.

LADY ŌTOMO OF SAKANOÉ AND ŌTOMO YAKAMOCHI, HER NEPHEW

If I sent my forlorn love
    On a pack-horse—a stout horse—
To your land of Koshi,
Would anyone be tempted,
I wonder, to cajole it away?—*By the Lady*

Should a horse-load of love
    Arrive from the Imperial City
When my love's daily stock
Is by no means exhausted,
I could not carry it, I fear.—*By Yakamochi*

LADY ŌTOMO OF TAMURA

To her sister, Lady Ōtomo of Sakanoé's Elder Daughter

At home the *hagi* flowers of autumn
    Are abloom in the evening glow—
Would that this moment
I could see your radiant form!

ŌTOMO YAKAMOCHI

Elegies on the death of his mistress, in summer,
in the sixth month of the eleventh year of Tempyō (739)

From this time on
    The autumn wind will chill me;
How shall I sleep alone
The long nights through?

Seeing the fringed pink by the stone-paving under the eaves

The fringed pink in my garden
    Which my beloved planted
For her remembrance in autumn-tide,
Has all come out in bloom.

In sorrow at the autumn wind in the following month

Well do I know that human life is passing;
    Yet this autumn wind chills me,
Reminding me of my lost love.

The flowers have blossomed in my garden,
    Yet do not soothe my sorrow;

If only my love were living,
Side by side could we be
Like a pair of mallards;
And I would pick them for her sake!
Brief is our lease of life,
She vanished like a drop of dew;
Seeking the mountain-side,
Like the setting sun she hid herself;
Remembrance wrings my heart.
Past speech the world is vain—
What can I do?

Envoys

Could she not have chosen another time?
To my grief she died, my love,
Leaving me a babe.

Had I but known the way she left our world,
I would have built a barrier
Between my dying love and death.

In the garden which my darling loved
The flowers still bloom;
And a long time has passed,
Yet my tears are not dry.

Still depressed in his sorrow

Such a fleeting life though we shared together,
    We both had trusted that our love
Would last a thousand years.

Once I saw it with uncaring eyes;
    Now that it is her sepulchre,
How dear it is, this hill of Saho!

Addressed to a young woman

Over the river ferry of Saho,
    Where the sanderlings cry—

When can I come to you,
Crossing on horseback
The crystal-clear shallows?

Having seen your smile
     In a dream by chance,
I keep now burning in my heart
Love's inextinguishable flame.

How I waste and waste away
     With love forlorn—
I who have thought myself
A strong man!

Rather than that I should thus pine for you,
     Would I had been transmuted
Into a tree or a stone,
Nevermore to feel the pangs of love.

To Lady Ōtomo of Sakanoé's Elder Daughter

Would there were a land
     Uninhabited by man!
Thither I'd take my love,
And happily we twain would live.

To the same

What pain and distress
     A dream tryst brings!
I start and wake,
And grope in vain for you,
Beyond the reach of my hand.

On the new moon

When I look up and gaze
     At the young moon afar

I remember the painted eyebrows
Of her whom only once I saw.

On the cicadas

Tired of sitting indoors all day long,
    I seek the garden for solace, only to hear
The shrill chirps of the cicadas.

On the cuckoo

In the leafy tree-tops
    Of the summer mountain
The cuckoo calls—
Oh, how far off his echoing voice!

On the cry of a deer

So loud the deer cries, calling to his mate,
    That the answering echo resounds
Through the mountains,
Where I am alone.

Sent with orange-blossoms to Lady Ōtomo of Sakanoé's Elder Daughter

While I waited and wondered,
    The orange-tree that grows in my garden,
Spreading out a hundred branches,
Has burst into bloom, as the fifth month
For garland-making draws near.
Every morning and every day I go out
To see the flowers and keep close guard,
Lest they should fall off
Before you, whom I love as the breath of life,
Have seen them once on a night when the moon
Is clear as a shining mirror.
But the wicked cuckoo,
Though I chase him again and again,

Comes crying in the sad hours of dawn
And wantonly scatters the blooms on the ground.
Knowing not what to do,
I have reached and broken off these with my hand,
Pray, see them, my lady!

Envoys

These are the orange-blossoms of my garden
I had intended you to see
Some time after mid-month
On a clear moonlight night.

The cuckoo has scattered
My orange-blooms on the ground.
Oh, had he only come
After you had seen the flowers!

To Lady Ōtomo of Sakanoé's Elder Daughter

Thinking sad thoughts over and over,
      I know not what to say,
I know not what to do.

You and I went out hand in hand
Into the garden in the morning,
While in the evening we brushed our bed
And lay together, our white sleeves overlapped.
Those nights—did they last for ever?
Though the copper-pheasant woos his mate,
They say, from an opposite mountain peak,
I, man that I am, if separated
Even for a single day or a single night,
Must long for you and grieve—ah, why?
I dwell on it, and my heart aches.

So, for healing I go forth
To Takamado and wander over hill and dale;
But there I find only the fair-blooming flowers
That remind me ever the more of you.
What can I do to forget this thing called Love?

Envoy

Ah, I cannot forget you—
In the *kao-bana* that blooms
In the fields of Takamado
I see your phantom face.

Love poems

My wife and I are one in heart:
        However long we are side by side,
She is charming all the more;
Though face to face we sit,
She, my cherished love,
Is ever fresh as a new flower,
Never annoying, nor vexing.
I, obedient to our Sovereign's word,
To rule the frontiers far-off as the skies,
Crossed the mountains and the plains,
Parting from my wife.
Since then the year has changed,
The spring flowers have fallen,
Yet never have I seen her.
So, forlorn and comfortless,
I sleep with my sleeves turned back;
And I meet her each night in my dream,
But as I cannot waking see her,
My longing grows a thousandfold.
Were I near enough, I would go
Even for a day's visit,
Lying in each other's arms;
But the way is all too far
And the barrier stands between.
Though that is so, yet I may hope—
Would that the month might quickly come
When the cuckoo cries!
And I might seek the Ōmi road,
And set sail upon the lake,
Gazing far upon the hills

Dotted with *unobana* bloom.
And there in Nara, at my home—
While, like the 'night-thrush,' she grieves,
Forlorn in her heart,
Asking the evening oracle at the gate,
And in sleep awaiting me—
I would hasten to my wife again.

Envoys

Though a year has passed
I have not seen her,
And my heart is heavy
With thoughts of my love.

Vainly I meet her in my dream,
But, waking, cannot see her face to face,
My longing but increases.

Though she is far away
Beyond the hills I crossed,
My thoughts reaching out to her,
Bring her to me in dream.

Though the spring flowers are gone,
I have not seen my love;
And she must wait for me,
Counting the days and months.

Wishing for pearls to send to his home in the capital

Of those abalone pearls
      That Suzu's fisher-maids dive for,
Crossing over, I hear,
To the holy isle of the sea,
Would I had many—even five hundred!
To my dear loving wife,
Who ever since we parted sleeves,
Must be sighing after me,
Counting the weary days and months
Passing the nights in a half-empty bed,

And forbearing to comb her morning hair—
To her I'd pack and send them,
Saying: 'Just to comfort you, darling,
Make a garland of these pearls,
Threading them together with orange-blossoms
And the sweet flag flowers of June,
When the cuckoo comes to sing!'

Envoys

How I wish to send home to my love
A package of those lucent pearls,
That she might string them together
With orange-blossoms and sweet flag flowers!

O for the abalone pearls
They dive for, I hear,
Crossing over to the holy isle of the sea!
I would pack and send them home.

O for the lucent pearls
From the holy isle of the sea,
That I might send them to my love
To comfort her heart!

How happy should I be,
Were there a fisher-maid to give me
Those shining pearls by the hundred,
Scooping them up in her hands!

Admonition to Owari Okuhi, a shishō of Etchū Province

Under the Seven Causes permitting Divorce the law says:
  For any one of these causes the husband may divorce his wife.
  But he, who in the absence of any of the Seven Causes wantonly
  casts his wife away, shall be liable to penal servitude for one year
  and a half.
Under the Three Cases prohibiting Divorce it says:
  In these cases the wife may not be divorced even if guilty of the
  offences under the Seven Causes.
  A violation of this provision is punishable by one hundred

strokes. *Only in the case of adultery, or foul disease, may she be cast away.*
Under Bigamy the law says:
A man who, having a wife, marries another woman, shall be liable to penal servitude for one year. The woman shall after one hundred strokes be separated from him.
The Imperial Rescript says:
Righteous husbands and faithful wives shall be accorded benevolence and bounties.

In my humble opinion the things cited above constitute the foundation of law and source of morality. Thus, the way of a righteous husband lies in constancy of heart. Man and wife live under one roof and share a common property. How can it be allowed that a husband should forget the old bond of love and form a new one? I have therefore indited the following short poem in order to make you repent of having forsaken your old ties.

Since the time of the gods
    Of Ōnamuchi and Sukunahikona
It has been said from age to age:
'To see one's parents is to revere them,
To see one's wife and children is to love them:
This is the law of the world of man.'
And so has it been told unto these days.
You who are a man of this world—
Have you not declared—did you not sighing say
In that full-flowering time of the *chisa*-trees,
While talking with your dear wife,
Morning and evening, 'mid smiles and tears:
'It will not be thus for ever.
The gods of heaven and earth helping us,
Some day we may prosper like spring flowers.'?
Now that prosperity has come which you longed for,
Your wife far away is waiting
In sorrow and in solitude,
Wondering when you will send for her.
Yet to that Saburu girl, who drifts
With no place to settle in like the foam
That floats on the swelling stream of the Imizu

When the south wind blows and melts the snow,
You cling inseparably like tangled twine.
Paired with her like the grebes,
You plunge into the depths of folly
Deep as the gulf of Nago, hopeless man!

Envoys

How deeply your wife must feel,
Who in the distant city of Nara
Is waiting—is it not so?—
Waiting on tiptoe for your messenger!

The townsfolk watch you from behind
When you go to the Government Hall—
What a shameless figure of a man
Infatuated with the Saburu girl!

Pink fades so quickly.
Better far, beyond comparison,
Are the long-accustomed clothes
Dyed in the grey of *tsurubami.*

On the arrival of the wife, who came by herself without waiting for a messenger from her husband

At the house where the Saburu girl
      Worships her lover,
There has arrived a post-horse without bells,
Upsetting the whole town.

Looking at the flowers in the garden

Since by the imperial order to serve
      At my Sovereign's distant court
I came to Koshi, the land of snow,
For five long years I have not laid
My head on your dainty arm,
But have slept in my clothes
With my girdle about me.
To console my sad weary heart

I have sown in the garden the fringed pink
And transplanted the lilies
Plucked from the summer plain.
Ah, but for the comforting thought they awaken
Every time I go out to see them in bloom—
The pink that so resembles you, my dear,
And the lily which spells 'afterwards'—
The thought that afterwards I shall see you again,
How could I ever live a single day
In this far provincial town?

Envoys

Every time I see the pink flower
I remember, dear girl,
The beauty of your radiant smile.

But for the hope of seeing you
'Afterwards,' as tells the lily,
How could I live through this one day to-day?

*On being asked by his wife for a poem
which she could send to her mother at the capital*

Like the orange-flowers that blow
      With the fifth month when the cuckoo calls,
Your voice is sweet to me, O mother.
But as many are the lonely days
I have lived in the country distant as the skies,
Where morning and evening I hear you not,
And as I look far towards the clouds
Arising from between the mountains,
I do not cease from grieving,
Nor do I cease from thoughts of you.
So, until I see your loving face
That I long to look upon,
Like the pearls the fisher-maids
Dive for in Nago Bay,
Flourish, my noble mother,
Like the pines and junipers.

Envoy

So long have I not seen you
Whom I long to see like the white pearls:
I scarcely feel alive,
Remaining in this distant land.

Composed after older poems on the tomb of the Maiden Unai

Told from age to age,
    It is a tale of long ago,
Wonderful as sad to hear,
That the young men, Chinu and Unai,
With their lives at stake
For the sake of their dear names,
Met in deadly strife
For the love of the Maiden Unai.
Then at the very bloom of her life,
Beautiful as flowers of spring,
Bright as the autumn leaf,
In pity for her lovers' suits,
Bidding farewell to her parents,
And away from home, at the seashore,—
When life is precious, even for so short a space
As the joint of the seaweed swaying in the eightfold waves
That flood with morn and eve—
She died, as vanish dew and frost.

So, here her tomb was built,
And for those who hear the story told,
That they may remember it for ever,
Her boxwood comb was planted
Which struck root and grew,
Ever, as now, thus sideways leaning!

Envoy

Her little boxwood comb, the maiden's memory,
Grows now as a tree,
Throwing shoot after shoot,
Ever sideways leaning.

An elegy

Since the beginning of heaven and earth,
　　Men of eighty clans have been set in office
Under our Sovereign's sway.
So, obedient to his word,
I crossed the hills and rivers
To rule the distant land.
Though wind and cloud may come and go
As couriers of my heart,
Many are the days
Since I saw you face to face,
And I long and sigh for you.
Then a traveller brought me word:—
That lately you have been sad at heart,
And you pass your days in grief.
The world is full of pain and sorrow,
The blooming flowers fade with time,
Inconstant is the life of man.
So your loving mother, at her age,
In the ripeness of her womanhood,
Alluring to the eye like a mirror—
As fades the mist that rises
And breaks the fresh-formed dew—
Drooped, like the swaying seaweed,
And is gone as goes the stemless stream.
Was it to deceive me?
Was it a trick?
But since I have heard it told,
Though faint as the distant twanging
Of the nail-flipped bowstring,
Sadness fills my heart,
And I cannot check my streaming tears
Like floods on the rain-beaten ground.

Envoys

When I hear, though from far away,
That you are bowed in grief,

I can but weep aloud,
I, your bosom friend.

You who know so well
How fleeting is our human life,
Do not wear out your heart,
You, a brave warrior!

Yakamochi wrote the above verses on the twenty-seventh of the fifth month of the second year of Tempyō-Shōhō (750), when his son-in-law, the second son of Fujiwara Toyonari, lost his mother.

Composed extempore, on the twenty-third of the second month of the fifth year of Tempyō-Shōhō (753)

Over the spring field trails the mist,
    And lonely is my heart;
Then in this fading light of evening
A warbler sings.

Through the little bamboo bush
Close to my chamber,
The wind blows faintly rustling
In this evening dusk.

Composed on the twenty-fifth day

In the tranquil sun of spring
    A lark soars singing;
Sad is my burdened heart,
Thoughtful and alone.

In the languid rays of the spring sun, a lark is singing. This mood of melancholy cannot be removed except by poetry: hence I have composed this poem in order to dispel my gloom.

LADY KI AND ŌTOMO YAKAMOCHI

For your sake, O slave,
    I plucked with busy hands

These sedge-buds from the spring meadow.
Eat them and grow fat!

The silk-tree that blooms in daytime
And sleeps the love-sleep at night,
Your lady should not see alone—
Look on this well, my slave!—*By Lady Ki*

With his lady your slave must be in love,
        For however much he devours
The sedge-buds so graciously given,
He wastes and wastes.

The silk-tree, my lady's precious keepsake—
Is it not, alas, a tree
That brings forth only the flower,
And bears not fruit?—*By Ōtomo Yakamochi*

ŌTOMO MOMOYO

Love poems

I have lived my life
        In peace and quiet—
Ah, that I should encounter
Now in my declining years
Love such as this!

When I shall have died of love—
What can avail me then?
I crave again to see you
While I live, dear lady.

YAMABÉ AKAHITO

Visiting Kasuga Field

On Mikasa, a peak of Mount Kasuga,
        Clouds hover every morning,
Kao-birds are for ever crying.
Like the clouds my heart is wavering;

And like the endless calling of the birds,
I long for love requited;
Every moment of the day,
Every moment of the night,
Standing or sitting,
I pine with thoughts of love
For the girl who will not heed me.

Envoy

Like the birds that call and call again,
On the height of Mikasa,
I only cease from weeping
To fall into tears.

HANISHI MITŌSHI

Composed at sea during his voyage from Tsukushi to the capital

As we go fast, rowing the huge ship,
 Should she hit the rocks and overturn—
Oh, let her overturn! I shall not mind
Since it is for my dear wife's sake.

YAMANOÉ OKURA

An elegy on the death of his wife

To this land of Tsukushi,
 Our Sovereign's distant court,
She followed me, my wife,
As a crying child its mother.
But before she gained her breath,
Ere many months had flown,
She sickened and lay dead,
When least I feared.
Now I know not what to do or say,
Vainly I seek soothing words
From trees and stones.
Had she remained at home,

Her form would still exist;
What means my heartless wife,
Breaking the vows we made
Side by side like grebes,
To wander from her home?

Envoys

When back at home, what shall I do?
How desolate I shall find
Her vacant bower!

Poor beloved!
Destined thus, she travelled far to me,
I cannot tell my grief!

How it fills me with regret!
Had I foreknown it, I would have shown her
All in this beautiful land!

The bead-tree's flowers my darling saw
Will be scattered
While my tears have not dried.

Over Mount Ōnu the fog is rising;
Driven by my sighs of grief,
The fog is rising.

Thinking of children

Buddha, from his holy mouth, truly preached, 'I love mankind as I love Rahula.' Again he preached, 'No love exceeds a parent's love.' Even so great a saint loved his child. Should not, then, the common run of men do so all the more?

When I eat melon,
    I remember my children;
When I eat chestnuts,
Even more do I recall them.
Whence did they come to me?
Before my eyes they will linger,
And I cannot sleep in peace.

Envoy

What use to me
Silver, gold and jewels?
No treasure can surpass children!

An elegy on the death of Furuhi

What worth to me the seven treasures,
    So prized and desired by all the world?
Furuhi, born of us two,
Our love, our dear white pearl,
With dawn, with the morning-star,
Frolicked about the bed with us, standing or sitting;
When dusk came with the evening-star,
He pulled our hands, urged us to bed,
'Leave me not, father and mother,
Let me sleep between you,
Like *saki-kusa*, the three-stalked plant.'
So spoke that lovely mouth.
Then we trusted, as one trusts in a great ship,
That he would grow up as time passed by,
And we should watch him, both in weal and woe.
But, as of a sudden sweeps the storm,
Illness caught our son.
Helpless and in grief,
I braced my sleeves with white cord,
Grasped my shining mirror,
And gazing up into the sky
I appealed to the gods of heaven;
Dropping my forehead to the ground
Madly I prayed to the gods of earth:
'It is yours to decide his fate,
To cure him or to let him die.'
Nothing availed my prayers,
He languished day by day,
His voice failed each morning,
His mortal life ebbed out.

Wildly I leapt and kicked the floor,
Cried, stared up, stared down.
And beat my breast in grief.
But the child from my arms has flown;
So goes the world. . . .

Envoys

So young he will not know the way;
Here is a fee for you,
O courier from the Nether World,
Bear him on your back.

With offerings I beseech you,
Be true and lead him up
Straight along the road to heaven!

A Seventh Night Poem

The Oxherd and the Weaver Maid standing
    Face to face across the River,
Since heaven and earth were parted—
Never has he ceased from loving,
Nor has he ceased from grieving.
Because of the blue waves all hopes are lost,
Because of the white clouds many tears have been shed.
Must he thus go on sighing?
Must he thus go on longing?
Had he a boat, vermilion-stained,
Had he an oar with a jewelled shaft,
He would ferry across in the calm of morning,
Or row over on the swelling tide of evening.
Then, on the shining beach of the Heavenly River,
The lovers would spread the celestial scarf
And lie, their beautiful arms interlocked,
In many a love-tryst, autumn though it be not.

Envoys

The wind and the cloud go to and fro
Between the banks—but no word comes
From his wife so far away.

Though it seems a stone's throw,
The Heavenly River separates them—
Nay, help there is none.

FISHER-FOLK OF SHIKA

Province of Chikuzen

Though, waiting for you to come,
    I put your rice in the bowl
And stand outside by the gate,
You come not home, Arao!

You care naught for the living
    Of your wife and children—
Though I wait these many years,
You come not home, Arao!

*In the era of Jinki the Dazaifu appointed Munakatabé Tsumaro,
a citizen of Munakata District, Chikuzen Province, steersman of
the ship carrying provisions to the island of Tsushima. Tsumaro
went to Arao, a fisherman of Shika Village, Kasuya District, and
said to him: 'I have something to ask of you.' Arao replied: 'Though
we belong to different districts, we have long sailed in the same
ship. To my heart you are dearer than a brother, and I am prepared
to share death with you. I will refuse you nothing.' Tsumaro said:
'The Dazaifu authorities have appointed me steersman of the ship
carrying provisions to the island of Tsushima. But I am too old and
weak to go to sea. Therefore, I have come to you. Will you take my
place?' Arao consented, and went to his work. Setting out from the
headland of Mimiraku, Matsura District, Hizen Province, he sailed
for Tsushima. Then, suddenly the sky grew dark, and a violent
storm broke out, attended with rain. Under the stress of weather,*

Arao went down with his ship. His wife and children, lamenting and longing for him, composed these poems. It is also said that Yamanoé Okura, then Governor of Chikuzen Province, who was touched by the plight of the wife and children, composed these poems in order to express their sentiments.

FROM THE "MUSHIMARO COLLECTION"

Of the Maiden Tamana at Sué of the province of Kazusa

There lived a maiden Tamana
    At Sué that bordered on Awa.
Broad of breast was she,
Her waist slender like a wasp's,
And radiant her face.

When she stood smiling like a flower,
Wayfarers, breaking their journey,
Turned to her door, unbeckoned.
A neighbour, abandoning his wife,
Unasked, offered his precious keys to her.

Thus charmed were all men;
And lithely she leaned upon them
With wanton airs and graces.

Envoy

When a man stood by her door,
Out she went and met him
Forgetting all,
Though in the dead of night.

Urashima of Mizunoé

When, in spring, the sun is misted,
    And going out on Suminoé's shore
I see rocking fisher-boats,
They remind me of the things
That happened long ago.

Urashima of Mizunoé
Went a-fishing to the sea;
Proud of his plentiful catch
Of sea-bream and bonito,
He did not come back home
Though seven days came and went;
But beyond the bounds of sea
He rowed out his little boat;
Then it happened that he met
The Sea God's daughter.
They talked, agreed, pledged love,
And hand in hand they reached
The Land Everlasting.

There in the Sea God's palace,
In its sweet and inmost chamber,
They might have lived, both he and she,
Never growing old, nor dying,
Until the end of time.
How foolish of this worldly man:
He said to his beloved:
'Let me go home for a while
And take word to my father and mother;
Then, again, as soon as it is morrow,
I shall come back to you.'
'If you will come again
To this Land of Happiness,
And meet me just as now,
Take this casket, but keep it closed.'
She said to him over and over.

Arriving at the shore of Suminoé
He sought his home, but could find none,
He sought his hamlet, which he could not see.
In wild wonderment he thought:
'In three years since I left,
How could my home be lost,
No trace of fence remaining?
If I open this casket,' he said,
'My old house may appear to me.'

Thereupon he opened it a little.
A white cloud rose out of the casket,
And drifted towards the Land Everlasting.

He ran, shouted, waved his sleeves;
He stamped and writhed upon the ground,
Then swooned upon the beach.
Wrinkles furrowed his youthful skin,
His black hair turned white.
His breath grew fainter and fainter,
At last he died.
That Urashima of Mizunoé,
I see the site of his abode.

Envoy

When he might have lived for ever
In the Land Everlasting,
How foolish of that man,
Though of his own choice!

Of a maiden walking alone on the great bridge of Kawachi

A maiden walks alone
    On the great vermilion bridge
Across the Katashiwa.

She trails her crimson skirt,
Her cloak is dyed blue
With the herbs of the mountain.

Has she a husband young as green grass?
Does she sleep single like an acorn?
I would ask her;
But, oh, not to know her bower!

Envoy

Were my dwelling by the bridge,
I would give her shelter,
So wistful she looks, going alone!

On climbing Mount Tsukuba

Climbing the peaks of Tsukuba
    Perchance to ease my heart, sorrow-laden
With travelling, grass for pillow,
I see the wild ducks are come,
Chillily calling in the fields of Shizuku
Where the 'tail flowers' fall,
And the land of Toba in Niihari
Is rippled white in the autumn wind.
And the splendid view from the peaks of Tsukuba
Relieves me of the heavy gloom
Gathered on many a weary day.

Envoy

As a gift for the comely maiden
Reaping in the autumn field,
Far down the Tsukuba Mountain,
Oh, I will break off a spray of tinted leaves.

Climbing Mount Tsukuba on the day of kagai°

On Mount Tsukuba where eagles dwell,
    By the founts of Mohakitsu,
Maidens and men, in troops assembling,
Hold a *kagai,* vying in poetry;
I will seek company with others' wives,
Let others woo my own;
The gods that dominate this mountain
Have allowed such freedom since of old;
This day regard us not
With reproachful eyes,
Nor say a word of blame.

°A colloquialism for *uta-gaki,* a popular festival in the eastern provinces during the course of which men and women danced together, singing amorous ditties.

Envoy

Though clouds upon the Male Peak rise
And autumn showers drench me through,
How can I leave it!

Of the Maiden of Mama of Katsushika

In the cock-crowing land of Azuma
          —As men have handed down to us
The tale of long ago—
It was a maiden Tekona
Who lived at Mama of Katsushika.
She wore blue-collared hemp,
And skirt of plain hemp-cloth that she wove;
She walked unshod, her hair uncombed,
And yet no high-born damsel dressed in rich brocade
Compared with this country girl.
When she stood smiling like a flower,
Her face like the full moon,
Many were the suitors seeking her,
As summer moths the fire,
As ships in haste the harbour.
Why did she wish to die
When life is but a breath?
She laid herself in her grave,
The river-mouth, under the noisy surf.
This is of the days long past,
Yet it seems that I had gazed
Upon her yesterday.

Envoy

When I see the well at Mama of Katsushika,
It reminds me of Tekona
Who stood here oft, drawing water.

On seeing the tomb of the Maiden Unai

The Maiden Unai of Ashinoya,
　　From her half-grown eighth year,
Until her loose-hung hair was done up,
Dwelt in safe seclusion,
Unseen by neighbouring folk.

Then many wooers gathered round,
Eager to see this lovely girl;
but two among them, Chinu and Unai,
Vied with each other for her smile.

They met, grasping their sword-hilts,
And with their quivers and bows of spindle-wood
Slung from their shoulders;
Each swearing in hot rivalry
To plunge through flood and fire.

Helpless, she sought her mother:
'When I see their deadly strife
Because of simple me,
How can I live to marry him I love?
I will wait in Yomi, the Nether World.'
So telling of her secret love for one
She killed herself in grief.

Chinu dreamed of it that night
And followed her in death.
Gallant Unai, left behind,
Cried in grief, looking up to heaven,
Ground his teeth and wept upon the earth;
Then bravely followed her with his sword,
'Never shall he defeat me!'

Their kinsfolk gathered in counsel,
And built the maiden's grave,
A tomb on this side and on that
For each hot youth;
As a token of their love for ever,
And a remembrance till the end of time.
Their history thus learned,

And though it happened long ago,
Moved me to tears
As if but now they had died.

Envoys

Whenever, passing through Ashinoya,
I see the Maiden Unai's tomb,
I weep and weep aloud.

The branches of the tree bend to one side
On the maiden's tomb;
It may be that her heart, some say,
Leaned to young Chinu so.

ATO TOBIRA, A YOUNG WOMAN

Once—only once,
      I saw him in the light
Of the sky-wandering moon;
Now I see him in my dreams.

TANIHA ŌMÉ, A YOUNG WOMAN

Here where the wild ducks
      Sport in the pond,
The leaves fall from the trees
And float—but no floating heart
Have I who love you true.

A YOUNG WOMAN OF HITACHI

*To Fujiwara Umakai when he left the province
for the capital upon his transfer to a new post*

Forget not, I pray, your Eastland girl
      Who will be thinking of you always,
As she cuts the hemp-stalks standing in the yard
And spreads them out to dry.

A YOUNG WOMAN OF HARIMA

*To the steward Ishikawa when he left for
his new post in the capital*

When you are away, wherefore should I adorn myself?
 Never shall I think of taking even the boxwood comb
Out of my toilet-case!

EMBASSY TO SHIRAGI

*Poems exchanged between the embassy despatched to Shiragi
and those who were left at home, expressing their sorrow at sepa-
ration, in the eighth year of Tempyō (736), and poems on the hard-
ships and solitude of the voyage*

When I am parted from you, my dearest,
 Who fold me as with wings,
As a water-bird its chick on Muko Bay,
On the sand-bar of the inlet—
O I shall die of yearning after you.

Could my great ship take you in,
 I would keep you, beloved,
Folding you as with wings!

When mist rises on the seashore
 Where you put in,
Consider it the breathing
Of my sighs at home.

When autumn comes we shall meet again;
 Then how should you raise such sighs
That they would mist the shore!

Wear yourself not out
 With yearning after me,
In the month when the autumn wind blows
We shall meet again.

For you, who journey to Shiragi,
      I will, in purification, wait,
Longing to see your eyes again,
To-day or to-morrow.

Unaware that the ships must wait
      For high tide,
I have parted, to my grief,
From my love so soon.

On the evening when they stopped at the shore of Kazahaya

My love must sigh after me—
      Far off from the shore of Kazahaya
A mist is trailing.

Referring to various things

From Mitsu, dearest shore to me,
      As to my wife her mirror in the morning,
We started at the flood-tide
In our stately full-oared ships
For the Land of Kara,
Steering straight ahead to Minumé
Piloted through the waves.

But the sea ran high with white surges
And we coasted shore after shore;
As evening drew on, clouds arose
And veiled the island of Awaji,
That made me long to see my love.

At dead of night, with our bearings lost,
We harboured in the bay of Akashi
And passed the night upon the water;
When far out at sea we saw
Fisher-maids row their little boats,
Floating them side by side.

As daylight came and the flood-tide reached us,
Cranes called flying to the reedy coast;
To leave the shore with morning calm,
Both our boatmen and rowers,
Laboured with loud cheers;
And like the grebes we pushed our way
To see the dim, far isle of 'Home.'

If the isle was faithful to its name,
It would relieve our weary hearts;
We strained and rowed our stately ships
To come to port the sooner,
But the sea rose up between.

We left the islet far away
And anchored ship at Tama;
Like a crying child we wept
To see the shore and the beach.

Here I have gathered for my wife
The gems that deck the Sea God's arms
And put them in my sleeves;
But what use are they
When I have no messenger
To take them home?
So I drop them down again.

Envoys

At Tama Bay I have gathered
The white pearls of the ocean,
But I drop them down again,
To no one can I show them.

When autumn comes
Our ships will harbour here;
Bear and leave shells of forgetfulness,
You, white surges of the ocean.

Three days after they had landed at Karadomari
in Shima District, Chikuzen Province, they looked at
an unusually beautiful moon, and, moved by the scene,
each composed a poem on the tedium of the journey. This poem,
one of six, was composed by Mibu Utamaro, the Daihangan

Although I am on a journey,
    I pass the evening by the blazing fire,
While my wife at home
Must long for me in the dark.

POEMS BY THE FRONTIER-GUARDS

Despatched from Various Provinces to Tsukushi as a Relief
Contingent in the Second Month of the Seventh Year
of Tempyō-Shōhō (755)

Presented to the Court by the Military Commissioner,
Sakamoto Hitogami, an official of Tōtōmi Province,
on the sixth day of the second month

My wife thinks of me much, I know;
    Her shadow shows in the water
Of the well-pool from which I drink—
For the world I can't forget her!
  —*By Wakayamatobé Mumaro, Aratama District;*
    a guard who was a district official

Even in a strange land I see
    The flowers of each season bloom—
The flowers I have known at home.
Why is it that there grows
No flower called 'Mother'?
  —*By Hasetsukabé Mamaro, Yamana District;*
    a guard

O that my father and my mother were flowers!
    Then, even if I must travel, grass for pillow,

I would take them with me,
Holding them reverently in my hands.
—*By Hasetsukabé Kuromasa, Saya District*

I wish I had the leisure
    To draw a picture of my wife
That I might look on it and think of her
As I go on my journey!
—*By Mononobé Komaro, Lower Naga District*

  *Presented to the court by the Military Commissioner of Suruga
Province, Fusé Hitonushi, on the seventh day of the second month*

Though I tried to forget, as I came
    Trudging over moors and over mountains,
I cannot forget them—
My father and my mother!—*By Akino Osamaro*

    *Presented to the court by the Military Commissioner
    of Kazusa Province, Mamuta Samimaro, on the ninth day
    of the second month*

Ah, must I leave you, dear—
    You, who clasp me,
Even as the creeping bean-vine clings
To the wild rose-bush by the wayside!
—*By Hasetsukabé Tori, Amaha District; a guard*

Well do I remember how she wept,
    Standing in the reed-fence corner—
That dear girl of mine—
Her sleeves all wet with tears!
—*By Osakabé Chikuni, Ichihara District; a guard*

When I started out from home
    In obedience to the imperial command,
How the girl clung to me
And moaned her grief!
—*By Mononobé Tatsu, Sué District; a guard*

*Presented to the court by the Military Commissioner
of Shimotsuké Province, Taguchi Ōto,
on the fourteenth day of the second month*

O for a sight once more
    Of my dear mother now—
When the ships are ready
By the shore of Tsu-no-Kuni,
And I go forth!
—*By Hasetsukabé Taruhito, Shioya District; a guard*

*Presented to the court by the Military Commissioner of Shinanu
Province on the twenty-second day of the second month*

At Misaka, the Pass of the Gods,
    I have made offerings,
Praying for the safety of my life—
All for my mother's and father's sake.
—*By Kamutobé Kooshio, Hanishina District; a guard*

ŌTOMO TABITO

Poems composed on a trip to the river of Matsura

Preface

*Once I wandered for a while in the district of Matsura. When I
visited the abyss of Tamashima, I happened to meet some girls fish-
ing. Their flowery faces and radiant forms were beyond compare.
Their eye-brows were like tender willow leaves, and their cheeks
were like peach flowers. Their spirits soared above the clouds, and
their gracefulness was not of this world. I asked, 'Where do you
live? What is your father's name? Are you, if I may ask, fairies?'
They answered, smiling, 'We are a fisherman's daughters. Being of
low birth, we live in a grass-thatched cottage. We have neither land
nor house of our own. How can we give you our names? But, by
nature we are kin with the water, and love the mountains. So, at
one time, at Lopu we vainly envy the life of the giant fish; at an-
other, lying at Wuhsia vainly do we look up to the banks of trailing
mists. Now, by rare chance, we have met with one so noble as you,
and we are happy to have revealed ourselves. So, will you pledge*

yourself to us for life?' 'Yes,' I replied, 'gladly I will.' Just then the
sun set beyond the western mountains, and my horse was impa-
tient to leave. Therefore I expressed my feeling in verse.

But a fisherman's daughters
    You say of yourselves,
Yet your looks reveal
That you are girls of noble birth.—*By Tabito*

On the Tamashima River,
Here by its upper stream, stands our home.
But from bashfulness
We did not tell you where.—*By the girls*

In the river of Matsura,
You stand fishing for *ayu,*
Brightening up the shallows;
Your skirts are drenched.—*By Tabito*

When spring comes round,
Through the ford near our home,
The little *ayu* will shoot,
Impatient for you.—*By the girls*

ANONYMOUS

The Scarf-Waving Hill

Ōtomo Sadehiko was suddenly despatched on a special mission
to the Sovereign's tributary. His sweetheart, Lady Sayo of
Matsura, sorrowing at this hasty separation, and in her fears of
never meeting him again, climbed a steep hill, and watched her
lover's ship sail away, her heart breaking with grief. At last she
took off her scarf and wildly waved it. At this, those who happened
to be near her burst into tears, and ever after people called the hill
the Scarf-Waving Hill.

Lady Sayo of Matsura, as her name tells
    Of one waiting for a lover far away,
Pressed by her longing, waved her scarf;
Hence the name of this hill.

ISONOKAMI OTOMARO AND HIS WIFE

On the banishment to Tosa of Isonokami Otomaro

Because of your errant love for a maid,
    Luckless Lord Furu Isonokami,
Bound with a rope like a horse,
And surrounded with bows and arrows
Like a hunted boar,
You go at the dread imperial command
Down to the province, heaven-distant.
Would from the mountain of Matsuchi
You could return to us who wait behind!

You set out, dear lord and friend,
In obedience to the imperial command,
For that land across the sea,
May the Gods of Suminoé who—
Though too awesome to speak of—
Appear in mortal shape,
Descend upon your ship's prow
To protect you from wind and wave,
At every island point you touch,
And every turn of the coast you pass!
May they keep you free from all ills
And shortly send you back to your homeland!

I, a dear child to my father,
    And a dear child to my mother—
Alas! on the 'Awesome Pass' of Kashiko
Where men of eighty clans
Returning to the capital
Make offerings with joyful thanks,
I present my *nusa* sadly in prayer,
Going down the long road to Tosa!

Envoy

Off the hallowed strand of Ōsaki,
Though narrow is the sound,
The boatmen thronging the water

Will not pass hastily on,
As I—alas! an exile—must.

ANONYMOUS

*Addressed to a son by his mother when the ships
of the embassy to China were leaving the port of Naniwa
in the fifth year of Tempyō (733)*

A deer that seeks the *hagi* flowers for mate
    Brings forth a single fawn, it is told;
My son, single as that fawn, now starts
Upon his travels, grass for pillow;
And I, purified, hang a string of bamboo-rings
And, setting out the sacred wine-jar
Dressed with mulberry cloth,
Implore the gods,
May he of whom I think
Ever travel safe and sound.

Envoy

When hoar-frost falls on the plain
Where the traveller shelters,
Cover my darling with your wings,
O flock of cranes of heaven!

ANONYMOUS

Shallow is the mountain well-pool
    That glasses the clean image
Of yonder hill of Asaka—
But no shallow heart
Have I for you, O Prince!

*Regarding the above poem it is said: On the occasion when
Prince Kazuraki was despatched to the province of Mutsu, the
Governor received him in a conspicuously neglectful manner. The
prince was displeased, and there was anger in his looks. Though
wine and food were offered him, he refused to touch them. Now*

there was in the company a former unemé (a palace attendant), who was an accomplished lady. Holding a wine-cup in her left hand, and wine in her right hand, she tapped the prince on the knee and recited this poem. The prince, appeased and delighted, made merry, drinking all day long.

ANONYMOUS

When the Governor-General of the Dazaifu, Ōtomo Tabito, was appointed Chief Councillor of State, and travelled home to the capital, in winter, in the eleventh month of the second year of Tempyō (730), his followers took a different route, going by sea. On that occasion they composed poems on the sorrows of the journey. The following is one of the ten anonymous poems.

Starting out on my travels,
    Unknown as the limit of the great sea,
She asked me when I should return,
That lovely girl!

ANONYMOUS

Cherry-Flower Maid

Once there was a young woman of the name of Sakura-ko (Cherry-Flower Maid). She was courted by two young men, who in their rivalry cared not for their lives, but contended bitterly as if eager for death. The girl wept and said to herself: 'From olden times to these days never has it been heard nor seen, that one woman should go to two houses to marry. Now there is no way to reconcile the hearts of these young men. It would be best for me to die so that they may cease for ever from harming each other.' Then, she sought the wood, where, hanging herself from a tree, she died. The two young men could scarce contain their grief. Tears of blood trickled down their collars. These are the poems they made to express their sentiments:

I thought I would wear it
    When the spring came—
Alas, my 'cherry-flower'
Is fallen and gone!

When the cherry-flower blooms—
My dear love's namesake—
I shall long for her
Each year and evermore!

ANONYMOUS

Once there was a young man and a fair maid (their names cannot be ascertained), who were meeting in secret, unknown to their parents. Now the maid, desiring to acquaint the parents with the affair, wrote a poem, and sent it to her lover.

Love is a torment
    Whenever we hide it.
Why not lay it bare
Like the moon that appears
From behind the mountain ledge?

ANONYMOUS

If need be, I'd follow you
    Even to the rock vault
In the Ohatsusé Mountains
And be together with you;
Be not troubled, dearest!

It is said that there was a young woman who met a young man in secret without letting the parents know of it. The young man, fearing their rebuke, seemed rather doubtful about continuing the affair. Thereupon, the young woman composed the above poem and sent it to him.

ANONYMOUS

If there be a law that allows
    The tradesman to break a contract,
Return to me, then, my under-robe!

It is said that there was once a young woman beloved of a high-born personage. His love waning, he returned to her the keepsake she had given him. Thereupon the girl, aggrieved and resentful, composed the above poem and sent it to her fickle lover.

ANONYMOUS

An elegy on the death of his wife

Are there no gods of heaven and earth?
    My dearest wife is dead!
Though I wished to live hand in hand
With my love, Hata-otomé—
Her name tells of the god
Who lightens and thunders—
All my hopes were vain!
And I am in despair.
With a sash of mulberry cloth on my shoulders,
And in my hands offerings of twill bands,
I prayed, 'Divide us not!'
Yet those sleeves of hers I slept upon
Now trail among the clouds!

Envoy

O that I could think it real!
No use: I only dream I lie
Pillowed on her sleeves.

AZUMA UTA (Eastland Poems)

Poems from the province of Hitachi

Though I have silks
    Fresh from the new mulberry cocoons,

Of the Tsukuba Mountain,
Oh, how I'd love
To wear that gown of yours.

On the Tsukuba Mountain slope
Has snow fallen?—or no?
Has she—my darling girl—
Hung out her clothes to dry?

Poems from the province of Shimofusa

Though it be the night when I make
    Offerings of the early rice
Of Katsushika,
I will not keep you, darling,
Standing outside the house.

Would there were a horse
That could travel with silent feet!
Then, over the jointed bridge of Mama
In Katsushika, I'd come to you
Night after night.

A poem from the province of Hitachi

As if with wardens posted
    On this and that side of the Tsukuba Mountain,
My mother watches me;
But our spirits have met.

Poems from the province of Shinanu

The highway of Shinanu
    Is a new-cut road.
You may trip on the stubs:
Put on your sandals, dearest!

Even the pebbles on the beach
Of the Chikuma River in Shinanu,
If you walk on them,
I will gather like precious stones.

Poems from the province of Kamitsuké

Let our love be made as plain
    As the rainbow that spans
The Yasaka weir of Ikaho,
Could I but sleep and sleep with you!

Do not rumble, O Thunder,
Over the mountains of Ikaho!
Though to me it is no matter,
You frighten this little darling of mine.

The mountain wind of Ikaho—
There are days when it blows
And there are days when it blows not.
But my love is timeless.

Poems from the province of Shimotsuké

O that I were the cloud
    That sails the sky!
To-day I'd go and talk to my wife;
To-morrow I'd come back again.

The cloud clings
    To the high mountain peak—
So would I cling to you, were I a cloud,
And you, a mountain peak!

Here at the river neck,
    With green-budding willows over-
grown,
Oh, how I wait for you—
No water I draw from the stream,
But stand, ever stamping the ground!

POEMS OF FRONTIER-GUARDS

A frontier-guard
    I set out in the morning;
And at the door—

How she wept, my darling wife,
Unwilling to let go my hand!

I will think of you, love,
        On evenings when the grey mist
Rises above the rushes,
And chill sounds the voice
Of the wild ducks crying.

When I see a woman
        Indifferently asking,
Whose husband is going
As a frontier-guard,
How I envy her lot,
So free from all cares!

O for the body of my darling wife,
        Better far than seven coats
Worn one over another,
When on a chilly night of frost
The bamboo leaves are rustling loud!

DIALOGUE POEMS

Had I foreknown my sweet lord's coming,
        My garden, now so rank with wild weeds,
I had strewn it with pearls!

What use to me a house strewn with pearls?
The cottage hidden in wild weeds
Is enough, if I am with you.

Since I had shut the gate
        And locked the door,
Whence did you, dear one, enter
To appear in my dream?

Though you had shut the gate
And locked the door,
I must have come to you in your dream
Through the hole cut by a thief.

I would make my way without a thought of you,
    But when I look up to the green-clad hills,
The azaleas are you, my lovely girl,
And you, my blooming girl, the cherry-flowers.
People would make you mine,
They would make me your own.
Even the rugged hills, if men so wish,
Will draw towards each other;
Keep true your heart!

Envoy

How can I rid my thoughts of love?
I pray to the gods of heaven and earth,
Yet ever does my love increase!

So it is, my dearest lover;
    As time goes, eight long years,
Beyond the term of childhood
When my tufty hair was clipped,
Beyond the bloom of girlhood
Thriving like the sprays of the orange-tree,
And secret like this stream
That runs beneath the sand,
I wait till I win your heart.

Envoy

I, too, have prayed to the gods
Of heaven and earth,
Yet love will have its way.

Where others' husbands ride on horseback
    Along the Yamashiro road,
You, my husband, trudge on foot.

Every time I see you there I weep,
To think of it my heart aches.

My husband, take on your back
My shining mirror, my mother's keepsake,
Together with the scarf thin as the dragon-fly's wing,
And barter them for a horse,
I pray you, my husband.

Envoys

Deep is the ford of the Izumi,
Your travelling clothes, I fear,
Will be drenched, my husband.

What worth to me my shining mirror,
When I see you, my husband,
Trudging on your weary way!

By her husband

If I get a horse, my beloved,
You must go on foot;
Though we tread the rocks,
Let's walk, the two of us, together!

To gather the wave-borne pearls
    On the shores of Ki,
My dearest lord has travelled far,
Crossing the mountains of 'Man and Wife';
When, standing by the roadside in the evening,
I tried to divine:
'When will he come home?'
Then came the oracle;
'Lady, your husband whom you await
Does not come to you,
Because he seeks the pearls

Borne by the ocean waves,
Because he gathers the white pearls
Washed by the ripples on the shore;
"Seven days at longest, it will take me,
At soonest, two."
So your husband said;
Do not lose heart, good lady.'

Envoys

With the aid of staff or none
Would I start to meet him,
But alas, I know not
Which way he comes!

Not straight,
But by this road to Kosé,
Treading the stony shore,
I have come,
In love's distress.

He passed the night with me,
And as day dawned
Opened the doors and left for Ki;
When can I have him back at home?

By her husband

Though my love, long standing at the gate,
May now have retired within,
Since she so loves me, I return.

FROM THE "COLLECTION OF ANCIENT POEMS"

Come to me, my dearest,
    Come in through the bamboo-blinds!
Should my mother ask me,
I'll say, 'Twas but a gust of wind.

On the cuckoo

In the Kamunabi Mountains—
    My old home,
Whither I, a young man, am bound—
There among the mulberry twigs at dawn,
And in the young pine-trees at eve,
Your voice is heard;
The village-folk fondly listen,
While the mountain echo replies—
Is it for love of your mate,
O cuckoo, that you cry
Through the midnight hours?

Envoy

Are you, too, O cuckoo,
A wanderer from home
And longing for your mate—
You, who in the Kamunabi Mountains
Cry far into the night?

On rain

Let no rain fall to drench me through;
    I wear beneath my clothes—
The keepsake of my loved one.

On grass

Susuki, growing along the way to my beloved,
    When I go to her,
Bend, O *susuki* on the plain!

On the koto

When I take the *koto,* sobs break forth;
    Can it be that in its hollow space
The spirit of my wife is hiding?

A love poem referring to the pearl

The white pearl, sunk under the deep sea,
    Though the wind blows and the seas run high,
I will not rest until I make it mine!

Referring to the grass

He who burns the sere weeds
    On the open plain in early spring—
Is it not enough!
Must he burn my heart, too!

Referring to the thunder

Like the flash and roar near the clouds of heaven,
    To see him awes me,
To see him not saddens me.

Elegy

How fortunate he is!
    Who, until his raven hair is grey,
Can hear his wife's soft voice!

On the cherry-flowers

Though your season is not over,
    Cherry-blossoms, do you fall
Because the love is now at its height
Of those who look on?

Referring to rain

Can only a spring rain so drench
    Your garments through?
If it rains for seven days,
Will you not come for seven nights?

Referring to the grass

My love-thoughts these days
        Come thick like the summer grass
Which soon as cut and raked
Grows wild again.

Referring to flowers

That you like me not
        It may well be—
Yet will you not come
Even to see the orange-tree
Abloom in my door-yard?

Referring to the sun

Even in the heat
        Of the blazing sun of June,
That cracks the earth's green face,
My tear-wet sleeves will not dry
Because I see you not.

To-night he makes his one journey of the year
        Over the Heavenly River, passing Yasu Beach—
He, the love-lorn Oxherd longing for his maid,
Whom he can never see but once a year,
Though from the beginning of heaven and earth
They have stood face to face across the Heavenly River.

This evening when the autumn wind arises,
Swaying the pennoned reeds, stalk and blade,
He in his red boat, many-oared
And gaily trimmed, bow and stern,
Buffeting the white waves of the Heavenly River
And crossing the swift and swirling waters,
Will come rowing—the lone Star-man—
Certain of the bliss
Of his young love's embrace.
So will he sate his year-long want

To-night, this Seventh Night of the Seventh Moon—
Strangely it thrills my heart!

Envoys

This is the night
When the celestial lovers meet
To undo, the one for the other,
Their girdles of *Koma* brocade—
Ah, that rapture in the skies!

I think of the happy river-quay
Where the Oxherd, rowing on
Across the stream,
Will come at last
To moor his little boat.

On the moon

As I sit worn and weary,
      Pining after you,
The autumn wind goes sighing
And low hangs the moon.

Referring to night

Though men say
      An autumn night is long,
It is all too brief
For unloading my heart
Of all its love.

The crickets chirp at my bedside—
      And how my heart aches!
I sit up, unable to sleep,
Thinking of you all the while.

Referring to snow

Having met you as in a dream,
      I feel I would dissolve, body and soul,

Like the snow that falls,
Darkening the heavens.

If you so heed your mother,
   All is lost—never could you and I
Fulfil our love!

If I come to her
   When she waits and waits,
Full of gladness she will beam on me—
I will hasten to that smile.

I have determined that my dear lord's name
   Shall not be revealed,
Even with my life at stake;
Never forget me!

If I come, surprising her,
   Full of gladness she will brighten;
Those eyebrows linger in my eye.

When I meet you,
   I cannot but conceal my face,
Yet, ever after, I desire
To see you, dearest lord.

You had better tell
   A more plausible tale;
Who upon earth, since what age,
Died for a girl he never had seen?

However much I beat him
   With my clenched fist,
That he may forget her face,
Never chastened is he,
This rascal love!

I will not comb my morning hair:
　　Your loving arm, my pillow,
Has lain under it.

I who have counted me for a strong man,
　　Only a little less than heaven and earth—
How short of manliness now that I love!

Standing or sitting,
　　I know not what to do.
Though I tread the earth,
My heart is in the skies.

To-night I am coming
　　To visit you in your dream,
And none will see and question me—
Be sure to leave your door unlocked!

The drum that the watchman beats
　　Tells the time of our tryst;
It is strange that he has not yet come.

The vivid smile of my sweetheart,
　　That shone in the bright lamp-light,
Ever haunts my eyes.

Were the Itada bridge to crumble
　　At Oharida,
By the cross-beams I would come to you;
Be not troubled, my love.

Unresting, like the people
　　Dragging logs for the palace
In the timber-forest of Izumi,
I long for you.

Soot-black as she is, like the shed
　　Where Naniwa people burn the reeds,
My wife is ever fresh to me.

At every trotting sound of a horse's hoofs,
    I rush out under the pine and look,
Hoping it may be you.

Leave me, O propitious spirits;
    Since my love has come to this,
What care I for useless life?

While with my sleeves I sweep the bed
    And sit up, lonely, awaiting you,
The moon has sunk.

No ways are left me now to meet my love;
    Must I, like the lofty peak of Fuji in Suruga,
Burn on for ever
With this fire of love?

Troubles are many in the path of a little boat
    Making for port through the reeds.
Think not I have ceased visiting you—
I who would come this very minute.

When the moon that shines
    In the far empyreal sky
Is no more—then, only then,
Shall cease this love of mine.

Never do I doubt your heart,
    From whose depths ocean-deep
You promised me your love.

Loath to pass by her gate,
    I have bound the grass stalks there.
Let stay the knot, O wind!
For I will come to see it there again.

Though I am chidden like a horse
    That crops the barley grown across the fence,

I love and love—
Never can I halt my thoughts of you!

At the upper course of the river
        People wash the tender herbs;
Like a straying leaf thereof, I would float down,
And reach the shallows near my love!

Well is the hill of Mimoro guarded;
        The staggerbush is in bloom at the foot,
Camellias are in flower at the top;
How beautiful she is,
A mountain that would soothe even a crying child!

With the ninth month when the thunder
        Rumbles and the sky is overclouded,
The autumn showers set in
Before the wild-geese come and call.

By the watch-house on the sacred fields of Kamunabi,
On the pond-dykes in the hedge-bound fields,
Many elm-trees intermingle
With the sprays of autumn tints.

With my little wrist-bells ringing,
Woman though I am,
On tiptoe I bend and break the sprays
And run to deck your locks with them.

Envoy

Sorrowing to see them alone,
The yellow leaves of Kamunabi,
I broke some off to bring to you, beloved.

Though there are men without number
        In this fair Land of Yamato,

My mind ever clings to you
Like a wistaria-vine,
My heart ever holds to you
Like a tender blade of grass,
And I shall pass this tedious night
Longing for a sight of you!

Envoy

Could I but think
There breathed another like you
In this fair Land of Yamato,
How should I so languish?

The Land of Yamato is a land
        Where matters fall as will the gods
Without lifted words of men.
It is so, yet I do lift up words:
Do not the gods of heaven and earth
Know my love-lorn heart?
As days and months have passed,
With loving my mind is troubled,
With longing my heart aches.
If never I meet him,
I shall languish
Till I die.
When I see him face to face,
Only then my pain will cease.

Envoys

Since I trust you as a sailor
His stately ship at sea,
However much I spend myself for your sake,
Regret I shall not know.

Now you leave the Imperial City
On your journey, grass for pillow,
When can I have you home again?

Since days of old it has been said:
    'Love brings trouble to our hearts.'
So it is said from mouth to mouth.
And, not sure of my maiden's mind,
Nor of the means whereby to learn it,
Pouring all my mind and soul out
Till my heart withers like cut rushes,
In secret and unknown
I shall feed my helpless love for her
While I have breath.

Envoy

Though she may not think of me like this,
Alas, I cannot forget her
Even for a moment!

The water at Ayuchi in Oharida—
    People draw it ceaselessly,
They drink it constantly;
Ceaselessly as they draw it,
Constantly as they drink it,
I love you, lady, with a love
Which will never cease.

Envoy

To cast away my love-thoughts
I know not how;
So long it is since I met you!

In that most wretched hovel
    Only fit for burning,
On the foul and ragged matting
Ready for the rubbish heap,
He sleeps, his own arm intertwined
With the vilest of vile arms

Which I would tear awry.
Yet, for him,
Each moment of the whole long day,
Each moment of the darkest night,
I weep and wail
Until the flooring creaks.

Envoy

It is I that burn my heart out,
My heart
That yearns for him!

That meadow* which my heart loved
    Was fenced in by a villager;
Since when I heard that it was done
I know not how to stand,
I know not where to sit;
Even in my own house,
As if on a journey,
My heart is seared with longing,
Nor can I cease from grieving;
And wavering as clouds of heaven,
Disturbed as the fence of reed,
Disordered as entangled hemp,
Without a thousandth part of my great love
Being known and understood,
I languish till I die!

Envoy

Peerless is the love I make,
And so lean I waste,
I must wear my girdle threefold round.

---

*The girl he loves is likened to the meadow where she lives.

Through the plain of Miyaké
    Treading the earth with your bare feet,
Breasting your way through the summer grass,
What sort of girl do you visit, my son?

But, Mother, you don't know her,
But you don't know her, Father.
Her tresses black as a mud-snail's bowels,
The way she wears those fluttering, *yū*-ribbons,
The way she wears her Yamato boxwood comb,
That beauteous maid,—my love.

Envoy

To her, kept secret from my parents,
Pushing by the summer grass I hasten,
Through the plain of Miyaké.

My love stands in my sight
    Across the stream,
And on this side stand I.
I do not cease from longing,
Nor do I cease from grieving.

O for a little vermilion boat,
And a pair of little jewelled oars,
That I might row across
And talk and talk with her!

The village-folk told me, saying:
    Your sweet husband whom you miss
Came from the hill of Kamunabi,
Now strewn with yellow leaves;
He rode a jet-black horse
And crossed the shallows seven;
Yes, lonely and wan he met us—
This they told me.

Envoy

Would that I had passed them,
Untold, unspeaking!
Oh! why did they tell me
Of my husband's plight?

In the land where white clouds hover,
    In the land where blue skies bend,
Among all the people under the clouds of heaven,
Is it I alone that long for him?
Since I alone thus miss my lord,
Filling heaven and earth with words of longing,
Is it with pining that my heart sickens?
Is it with thinking that my heart aches?
My love increases with the days;
Ceaselessly I languish for my husband,
Yet, this ninth month which he told me
To keep as our never-to-be-forgotten month—
To recall for a thousand ages,
And talk of through eternity—
This ninth month, when our love began,
Fast races to its close;
How can I bear an agony so great?
For me the month is dying
To leave me in despair.
So, on the steep and rocky path,
To the rock-bound doorway
With morning I go out in grief,
With evening I come in, weeping;
And spreading out my jet-black hair I lie;
Not for me the soothing sleep of others,
Uneasy as a boat tossing on the waves,
With sorrowful thoughts I pass
Dreary nights numberless!

When I trusted as one trusts in a great ship,
    That he would come to me this month,

And I waited for the day,
A courier brought me word—
Though vague as a fire-fly's light—
That he was gone like the autumn leaf.
Now I tread the earth as flames,
Standing or sitting I know not where to go;
Bewildered like the morning mists,
Vainly I breathe out eight-foot sighs.
I would, to find him where he lies,
Wander as a cloud of heaven,
And die as the stricken deer,
But, as I do not know the way to him,
Thus I remain alone and miss him,
And weep aloud.

Envoy

When I see the wings of the wild-geese
Skimming the reedy shore,
They remind me of the arrows
He carried on his back.